HIDDEN FROM VIEW

24 MYSTERIOUS DISAPPEARANCES

JENN BAXTER

All rights reserved. No parts of this book may be reproduced or transmitted in any form, including photocopying, recording, or by any other information storage and retrieval system without permission in writing by the author. The only exception allows reviewers to copy or quote brief portions along with the book's title.

ISBN: 9798301890543
Copyright © 2024 by Jenn Baxter

In memory of Diva...my canine muse gone far too soon

CASES:
1. AMY BECHTEL
2. WESLEY BILLINGSLY
3. NORINE BROWN
4. KELLIE BROWNLEE
5. STEVEN CHAIT
6. SHAWN DICKERSON
7. TIFFANY DIXON
8. ROGER ELLISON
9. MARGARET FOX
10. ALI GILMORE
11. MARTHA LEANNE GREEN
12. ANGELA HAMBY
13. ANGELA HAMMOND
14. ALLAN KAPLAN
15. TRACY KROH
16. JASON LANDRY
17. CLAUDIA LAWRENCE
18. JUDY MARTINS
19. SHIRLEY MCBRIDE
20. WESLEY MORGAN
21. DENISE PFLUM
22. JAMES MARTIN ROBERTS
23. DOROTHY SCOFIELD
24. CARLIENE TENGELSEN

AMY BECHTEL

Amy Bechtel had a list of things she wanted to get done when she left her Lander, Wyoming home around 9:30 am on Thursday, July 24, 1997. The 24-year-old spent several hours checking items off her to-do list, and at 2:30 pm she went to a local photography shop to ask about getting some pictures framed. When Amy left the shop, she planned to go for a run so she could map out the route for an upcoming race she was organizing in the Shoshone National Forest. She never made it back home and she was never seen again.

Amy's husband, Steve Bechtel, had gone rock climbing with a friend that day and was somewhat surprised when he got home late that afternoon and Amy wasn't there. At first, he thought she might have gotten a late start on her run, so he waited for a couple of hours to see if she returned. When there was no sign of her by the time it started to get dark, Steve started calling some of their friends, but none of them had seen Amy that day and didn't know where she might be.

By 10:30 pm, Steve was growing increasingly concerned that something had happened to Amy. It was unlike her to be out of contact for an extended period of time, so he decided to call the police and report her missing. While he waited for officers to respond, two of the couple's closest friends drove along the route Amy would usually follow when she went running to see if they could see any sign of her or her car.

Shortly after midnight, Amy's car was found parked

along the loop road near Burnt Gulch in the Wind River Mountains. The car was unlocked, and most of her belongings, including her handwritten to-do list and car keys, were found inside the vehicle; the only thing that was missing was her wallet and fanny pack. There were no signs of foul play in or around the vehicle; it looked as if Amy had parked it there to go on her run and then never returned.

Fearing that Amy had injured herself while she was running, Steve and several of his friends spent the night searching the area for any sign of her. Steve was sure they were going to find her on the side of the trail, perhaps suffering from a broken leg. As hours went by, however, it became clear that Amy wasn't anywhere along her planned route.

The Fremont County Sheriff's Department launched a large-scale search for Amy on Friday. Search dogs, helicopters, and dozens of volunteers assisted in the search effort, but they were unable to find any trace of Amy. Dogs followed Amy's trail for three or four miles away from her car, then doubled back and left the main road, indicating that Amy may have taken a different route to return to her car. They lost the trail on a small side road; it was unclear if something had happened to Amy there or if the dogs had gotten confused.

The search effort was expanded over the weekend. Searchers used horses and ATVs to scour the backcountry while the Civil Air Patrol conducted an aerial search using infrared radar, hoping to spot a heat signature that could lead them to Amy's location. Rain, thunder, and hail moved into the area Sunday afternoon, hampering the search. Temperatures that night dropped into the 40s, making it imperative to find Amy before she succumbed to hypothermia.

Fremont County Sheriff's Deputy Brian Klein told reporters that although foul play hadn't been ruled out, they hadn't found any indication to suggest it had taken place. He also noted that there were bears in the area where Amy had parked her car, so they had to consider the possibility that she might have been attacked by one. By Sunday night, however, they hadn't found any evidence of a bear attack.

On Monday, officials asked for anyone who had been on Loop Road near Lander on the day Amy went missing to contact them; they were hoping someone might have witnessed something useful to the investigation. Fremont County Sheriff Larry Matthews admitted that they still had no idea what had happened to Amy. "Since we haven't found a darn thing, [foul play] is a possibility...all the options are open."

Everyone in Lander was on edge after Amy's disappearance, and as days went by without any sign of her, their concern grew. Ernie Over, the editor of the Lander State Journal, noted, "The longer this goes, everyone's worst fears bubble to the surface." Amy was well-known in Lander, where she taught classes at the Wind River Fitness Center and helped run the Wild Iris climbing and outdoor shop. Mattie Sheafor, a manager at Teton Mountaineering, stated, "She is one of the sweetest people I've ever met in my life."

A week after Amy was last seen, officials announced that they were going to start scaling back the search effort. Kim Lee, the emergency management coordinator for Fremont County, told reporters, "We've just exhausted all of our areas...we've searched the area thoroughly for clues...they are few and far between."

Sheriff Matthews admitted that there was a possibility that Amy had been abducted, and if investigators believed that this was what had happened, they would expand the search to include areas where someone might hide a body, including abandoned cabins and old mines. Steve told reporters that he had reached the point where he hoped Amy had been abducted because then there was a chance she was still alive; if she had been injured while running, he knew she couldn't have survived a week out in the elements.

Around 30 detectives were assigned to work Amy's missing person case. They started by interviewing her family and friends to see if they could offer any insight into her life at the time of her disappearance. Everyone they spoke to agreed that Amy wasn't the kind of person who would have vanished voluntarily; she loved her job and had a close relationship with her husband, parents, and siblings. It was completely out of character for her to be out of contact with her loved ones for any length of time.

The Wyoming Department of Criminal Investigation sent around two dozen agents to assist in the search for Amy. They brought a portable crime lab to Lander and started to process Amy's car for forensic evidence. They had moved away from the theory that Amy had gotten injured or lost while running and were concentrating on the possibility of criminal activity. Investigator Dave King noted, "We don't think Amy's on the mountain and that we've overlooked her. We're pretty confident in the search we've conducted."

Amy should have been celebrating her 25th birthday on August 4, 1997; instead of having a party, her loved ones continued their efforts to find her. Hoping to bring in some new leads, they announced that Crime Stoppers was offering a $10,000 reward for information leading to Amy's whereabouts. Tom Sanchez, who met Amy more than a decade earlier through the running community, added a $5,000 reward of his own, bringing the total amount available to $15,000.

Steve was hopeful that his wife was still alive. "We're scared and we're worried, but there's no reason for us to be distraught, because we don't have proof either way at this point." He and the rest of Amy's family members were kept busy with the search effort; they refused to give up until Amy was found.

After receiving reports from woodcutters about a suspicious smell near Louis Lake in the Shoshone National Forest, deputies and search dogs were dispatched to the area to see if they could find anything. The area was roughly 15 miles away from where Amy's car had been found and had been part of the initial search effort, but deputies spent two days going back over the area for any new clues. They found a deer carcass but nothing relevant to their investigation.

Two weeks after Amy went missing, investigators converged on the home she shared with Steve, searching it and Steve's pickup truck for any potential evidence. Sheriff Matthews refrained from naming Steve a suspect in his wife's disappearance, but told reporters that everyone who knew Amy was considered a potential suspect at this point in their investigation. "We're just looking for any clue we can get our hands on."

Steve told reporters that while having someone search his home wasn't a comfortable experience, he understood why it was necessary. Although he had initially cooperated with investigators, during one interview with detectives and FBI agents, one of the agents accused him of killing his wife. He left the interview and hired a lawyer. He was then asked to take a polygraph examination but declined on the advice of his lawyer.

Those who knew Steve and Amy well jumped to

Steve's defense, insisting that there was no way he had been involved in his wife's disappearance. In addition to having a solid alibi – he had been rock climbing with a friend in a different county at the time Amy went missing – friends said they had a solid marriage and were very much in love. They had recently closed on a new home and had been in the process of moving when Amy vanished, and they had been looking forward to their future together. Friends noted that by concentrating on Steve simply because he was the husband, police were allowing the true perpetrator to remain at large.

Sheriff Matthews admitted that the search of the Bechtel home hadn't found any incriminating evidence; there was nothing to suggest that Amy had been harmed inside the house. He said detectives hadn't really expected to find anything to incriminate Steve but had needed to search the home in order to be as thorough as possible in their investigation.

While the sheriff stated that Steve's refusal to take a polygraph examination was hindering investigators from ruling him out as a possible suspect, he did say that others, including Amy's father and brother, had been ruled out and were not considered suspects in her disappearance.

As the investigation entered its second month, some members of the Teton County Search and Rescue team admitted that the fact that her friends had found her car and conducted a search of the area might have inadvertently destroyed evidence. By walking along the path Amy was believed to have taken, they likely trampled over any of her footprints that might have been in the area. No one was blaming them – they did so with the best intentions – but it was a hindrance to the criminal investigation.

By the first week in September, detectives had

interviewed more than 350 people but had been unable to develop any solid leads and had no idea what had happened to Amy. When they learned that the Russian space station had been over the Lander area on the day Amy vanished, the FBI requested copies of any satellite images that had been taken. Unfortunately, they weren't of any use.

Detectives received several reported sightings of Amy in the Salt Lake City, Utah area, but they were unable to confirm them. Other sightings came in from New Mexico and Colorado, but it was believed that the witnesses saw someone who simply looked like the missing woman.

By the middle of September, those closest to Amy were starting to fear the worst. The reward for information had been increased to $50,000, but no new leads had been developed. Amy's parents and siblings started to believe that Steve might know more than he was saying – they were bothered by the fact that he wouldn't submit to a polygraph examination – and their suspicions drove a wedge between the family and Steve. Amy's parents, Duane and Joanne Wroe, as well as her brother, Nels Wroe, were vocal about their desire for Steve to take a lie detector test, but he continued to refuse.

While detectives still refrained from calling Steve a suspect in his wife's disappearance, they said that some of his poetry had been seized during the search of his home and they were concerned about some of his more violent writings. Steve explained that he had been in a punk band when he was younger and that his songwriting had nothing to do with reality, but this did little to reassure Amy's family.

Nels said he suspected that his sister had been a

battered woman, and Steve's violent songs were "flat-out shocking and consistent with what I've been suspicious of for a long time." Steve denied the claims and insisted that he and Amy had a great marriage. "We were never physically violent towards each other. Ever."

On September 28, 1997, Steve organized a 10K race to raise money for the search effort. The race covered part of the course Amy had followed on the day she went missing. An entry fee of $12 was charged, and donations were also accepted. All proceeds went to the Amy Wroe Bechtel Recovery Fund. Steve told reporters, "We doing the race out of honor for Amy, plus it keeps an awareness up that she is still missing."

Three months after Amy was last seen, investigators conducted a search of several old mine shafts in Atlantic City, Wyoming but found no evidence to suggest Amy was in that area. Sheriff Matthews said that the search hadn't been prompted by any specific information but the mines hadn't been searched during the initial investigation and detectives wanted to cover all their bases.

By the end of the year, there had been no progress on the case and the investigation was starting to stall. Detectives still had no idea what had happened to Amy after she set off on her jog, but they believed she met with foul play. The FBI spent months trying to locate a man who had been obsessed with Amy when she worked at a Lander café, but they were unable to place him in the area on the day she went missing.

By February 1998, the reward for information leading to Amy's recovery or the person responsible for her disappearance reached $100,000, but tips were starting to dry up and detectives had no solid leads to follow. Investigators continued to say that Steve's refusal to take a lie detector test was obstructing the investigation, but friends worried that detectives had developed tunnel vision and were focusing only on Steve while ignoring the fact that Amy's abductor was still free.

Steve's lawyer insisted that his client had provided detectives with a detailed account of his whereabouts on the day his wife went missing; the attorney also told reporters that he would not allow Steve to take a polygraph because they were unreliable, inadmissible in court, and prone to false positives.

Years went by and Amy's fate remained a mystery. Her disappearance was featured on both "Unsolved Mysteries" and the television show "Disappeared," resulting in a number of tips. Each one was followed up by detectives but none resulted in any new developments. The case stalled and went cold.

While there were still some people in Lander who believed that Steve played a role in Amy's disappearance, no evidence to support this theory ever emerged. It seems more likely that she was abducted and killed by a stranger. Years after Amy went missing, the public would learn that a man named Richard Eaton called detectives and told them that he thought his brother, Dale Wayne Eaton, was responsible for abducting and killing Amy. At the time, detectives seemed intent on going after Steve and it's unclear if this lead was adequately investigated.

Dale Wayne Eaton was arrested after he attempted to kidnap the Breeden family from Interstate 80 in Wyoming in September 1997. His brother told police that Dale had been camping in the Burnt Gulch area at the time Amy went missing, but his niece claimed he had been staying with her and couldn't have had anything to do with Amy's disappearance. Detectives chose to believe the niece and never questioned Dale about Amy.

In 2004, Dale was convicted of the 1988 murder of Lisa Kimmel; Lisa had been abducted from a rest stop in Waltman, Wyoming while she was on the way to her boyfriend's house. Her murder went unsolved for years until DNA taken while he was in jail for kidnapping linked Dale to the crime. Despite this, detectives still never attempted to interview him about Amy's disappearance.

It wasn't until cold case investigators started looking at the case in 2010 that the tip about Dale Wayne Eaton was reviewed again; detectives decided it was time to visit Dale in prison and see if he would tell them anything about Amy. Dale refused to speak about the missing woman, however, and remains a person of interest.

As of this writing, Amy's case remains unsolved. While all those involved in the investigation believe she is dead, since her body hasn't been found her case is still considered a missing person case. Until her killer starts talking – or her body is found – her fate remains a mystery.

Amy Joy Wroe Bechtel was just 24 years old when she went missing while jogging in Lander, Wyoming in July 1997. She was a sweet and friendly young woman who loved running and taught fitness classes in Lander. Amy and her husband had been married for a little over a year when she vanished; although he was initially a suspect, detectives are now unsure if he had any involvement in her disappearance. Dale Wayne Eaton has recently emerged as a more viable suspect but has refused to speak about Amy's case. Amy has blue eyes and blonde hair, and at the time of her disappearance, she was 5 feet 5 inches tall and weighed 110 pounds. She was last seen wearing a yellow tank top, dark-colored shorts, Adidas running shoes, a gold wedding ring, and a Timex Ironman Triathlon watch. If you have any information about Amy's disappearance, please contact the Fremont County Sheriff's Office at 307-332-5611.

WESLEY BILLINGSLY

Wesley Billingsly was a little down on his luck in 2018. The 24-year-old had lost his job at an advertising agency and hadn't been able to find a new job right away. When he was unable to come up with his share of the rent for the San Diego, California apartment he shared with roommates, he was asked to move out. Wesley knew he couldn't afford to get another apartment; he started staying with three different friends, bouncing back and forth between their homes. Friends recalled seeing him in Pacific Beach, California on June 12, 2018, but then he seemed to vanish without a trace.

Wesley arranged to meet some friends for dinner on the evening of June 12, 2008, but he didn't show up and didn't call them to say he wasn't coming. When they tried to call his cell phone, all their calls went straight to voicemail; it appeared Wesley had either turned his phone off or the battery was dead.

On June 13, 2018, Wesley had arranged to help some of his friends move. Once again, he failed to show up and didn't call to offer an explanation. All calls to his phone continued to go to voicemail, and he didn't call or text anyone back. Eventually, some of Wesley's friends let his mother know that they hadn't been able to get in contact with him. She called the San Diego Police Department and reported him missing.

Christel Billingsly, Wesley's mother, feared the worst and pleaded with the public for help. "He's never done this and it's now like he dropped off the face of the earth...we're searching for him...I don't know where he is but I need to know where my son is." She said he hadn't posted anything on social media, which was unlike him. Normally, he would post things multiple times a day, so the fact that he hadn't accessed his account was extremely concerning.

Prior to his disappearance, Wesley had been in frequent contact with his friends and family members. When he suddenly stopped answering his phone, everyone noticed. Christel noted, "It's not like Wesley...he is in constant contact with his family. His brother and myself, every couple of days...it just stopped."

Wesley's black Ford Expedition was also missing, and police sent out an alert so patrol officers would know the vehicle was associated with a missing person. Christel hung around 500 posters in Pacific Beach and the area around San Diego University, but investigators hadn't received many leads and weren't sure if Wesley was missing voluntarily or had been a victim of foul play.

The fact that Wesley's vehicle was missing concerned Christel. "Has somebody stolen his truck and dumped him somewhere? Something in my gut tells me something is wrong." She noted that she had been through hard things in her life, but nothing compared to her son's disappearance. "This is a nightmare."

Wesley had grown up in Sacramento, California, and moved to San Diego after high school to attend college. He graduated from San Diego State University in 2016 with a degree in business and marketing. He returned to Sacramento after graduation and lived with his mom for a while to save money, but moved back to San Diego in February 2018 after getting a job at an advertising agency.

When he lost his job, he didn't have the financial

resources to support himself but seemed reluctant to return to Sacramento. He didn't tell his mother that he was no longer working, likely because he didn't want to worry her. She was also unaware that he had been kicked out of his apartment and was crashing with friends.

Detectives noted that the investigation was complicated by the fact that Wesley didn't have a permanent address; he was bouncing back and forth between three different apartments, making it more difficult to pinpoint where he had last been seen.

Investigators said that they had interviewed several of Wesley's friends as well as his relatives, but no one had been able to provide any clues to his whereabouts. Everyone they spoke with said that it was highly unusual for the normally social Wesley to simply drop out of sight; while they didn't have any evidence of foul play, it was clear that Wesley wasn't the type to voluntarily disappear.

Two months after Wesley was last seen, his mother was growing increasingly desperate to hear from him. She offered a $3,000 reward for information leading to his whereabouts. "I was asking people to come forward out of the goodness of their hearts but I guess that doesn't work so I put money on it…I will give you the money if you tell me where my son is or where his truck is. I need to know what happened to him. Somebody knows."

Officials with the San Diego Police Department stated that they found Wesley's car two months after his disappearance, but were tight-lipped about any potential clues it contained. It had been abandoned on a street in the South Bay section of San Diego. While some of Wesley's personal belongings were inside, there was no sign of the missing man.

Wesley should have been celebrating his 25th birthday on August 17, 2018. Instead of buying gifts for her son, Christel drove to San Diego from her home in Sacramento, California to distribute missing person flyers and plead with people for help finding Wesley.

In case Wesley made his way across the border into Mexico, Christel spent some time searching for him there. With the help of a translator, she filed a missing person report with Mexican officials and checked Mexican jails and morgues. She didn't find anything to suggest that Wesley was in Mexico.

Nine months after Wesley vanished, Christel was still stalking the streets of San Diego, desperate for any information about what had happened to her son. She concentrated on areas he was known to frequent, such as the Vons supermarket on Garnet Avenue in Pacific Beach; she made sure every telephone pole in the area had a copy of his missing poster prominently displayed. "I try to keep hopeful, but nine months is a really long time."

Christel believed that there were likely people in the area who knew what happened to Wesley but were afraid to come forward with that information. "But this is my child...I would hope they would think of their mom, or their brother, or their uncle...it's just not okay."

Hoping that he would reach out to someone, Christel continued to pay for Wesley's cell phone so his phone number would remain active, but a check of his phone records showed that he hadn't used it since before he went missing.

As the first anniversary of Wesley's disappearance approached, Christel made another plea for help locating him. She also spoke directly to her son, telling him she missed him and just wanted him to come home. "I'm gonna keep searching, I'm gonna keep putting it on the news, I'm gonna keep knocking on doors, I'm gonna keep handing out cards, I'm gonna keep posting it on

Facebook."

As of December 2024, Wesley is still missing and detectives still have no idea what happened to him. There have been a number of theories and rumors about the case but nothing has helped lead investigators to Wesley. His mother continues to actively search for him, and there is currently a $10,000 reward for information leading directly to Wesley's location.

Wesley Keith Billingsly was just 24 years old when he vanished from the Pacific Beach area of San Diego, California in June 2018. His 2001 Ford Expedition was found two months later in the South Bay area; the vehicle contained some of Wesley's belongings but no clues to his whereabouts. Wesley has hazel eyes and brown hair, and at the time of his disappearance, he was 5 feet 8 inches tall and weighed 135 pounds. If you have any information about Wesley, please contact the San Diego Police Department at 619-531-2000 or 619-531-2777. There is a reward for information leading directly to Wesley.

NORINE BROWN

Norine Brown left her home in New Hyde Park, New York around 11:00 pm on Wednesday, December 12, 1990. The 31-year-old wanted to go to a nearby supermarket to buy some ingredients she needed to bake Christmas cookies. She preferred to go to the grocery store late at night to avoid crowds; she waited until her two young children were sound asleep and told her husband, John, that she would be back shortly. Norine grabbed some cash and climbed into her station wagon, leaving her wallet at the house. She never returned and she was never seen again.

Norine's husband, who was a New York City firefighter, said that he fell asleep on the couch and didn't realize that his wife failed to come home Wednesday night. When he woke up at 5:00 am Thursday, he saw that Norine never returned. He called Norine's good friend, Elaine Commando, and asked if Norine had spent the night with her. He claimed they had an argument before she left to go to the grocery store and he thought she might have visited her friend to calm down. Elaine hadn't heard from her.

Elaine later admitted that she felt slightly uneasy when she got John's phone call. Norine was a devoted mother who usually remained in constant contact with her loved ones. It was unheard of for her to simply disappear, even for one night. Still, Elaine wasn't overly worried. "At that point, I thought maybe she stayed at another friend's house. I wasn't too concerned."

Since John didn't want to leave the kids, he asked Elaine if she would drive to the nearby Pathmark and see if Norine's car was there. Elaine immediately drove to the grocery store and found the station wagon in the supermarket's parking lot. There was no sign of Norine.

The discovery of her friend's car sent Elaine into a panic. Elaine went back to her home and called John to tell him what she had found. He then called the police and reported his wife missing on the day she should have been celebrating her 32nd birthday.

Although those who knew Norine tried to explain their fears to the police, officers insisted that she couldn't be reported missing until she had been gone for at least 24 hours. The next day, when there was still no sign of the missing mother, police agreed to file a missing person report.

Investigators spoke with employees at the Pathmark and determined that one employee had seen Norine's car in the parking lot shortly before 11:00 pm while another saw it at 2:00 am. It was unclear if it had been in the parking lot the entire time or if it had left and then returned. None of the employees recalled seeing Norine.

When Norine's station wagon was found, it was locked and there were some Christmas presents that she had already wrapped in the backseat. The Pathmark, which was in Garden City Park, was less than a mile from the Brown's home and Norine regularly shopped there late at night. She had never mentioned any concerns for her safety in the parking lot at night.

At the time of her disappearance, Norine had two young children; Alexa, who was five months old, and Anthony, who was 18 months old. No one who knew her believed that she would have willingly walked away from her children, but close friends acknowledged that her marriage was troubled.

Norine and her two children had spent Wednesday with her sister, Susan, and Susan's new baby. They were starting to get into the holiday spirit; they took the children to have their picture taken with Santa Claus and did some Christmas shopping. Norine dropped her sister off at her house when they finished their shopping and told her that she was going to take her kids straight home. She had been in a good mood at the time and there was no indication that anything was wrong.

Elaine, who found Norine's car, later admitted that she thought John had something to do with his wife's disappearance. She pointed out that the parking spot where Norine's station wagon had been left was some distance from the entrance to the grocery store and likely not one that Norine would have chosen. "I'm not sure why she would park in that spot at 11:00 pm. She probably would have parked closer to the store."

In the days following Norine's disappearance, there were several organized searches for her. Her friends distributed missing person flyers throughout Long Island and volunteers combed through the area. Since John was a firefighter, he rallied many of his co-workers to assist in the search. Police canine units attempted to pick up Norine's trail but came up empty.

Desperate to find Norine, some of her friends decided to speak with a psychic to see if they could come up with any new areas to search. The psychic believed that Norine's body would be found in a Bronx park, so Elaine and several other friends went there and combed through the park. They found nothing.

Maria Przybylski, one of Norine's close friends, admitted that those who knew Norine weren't optimistic about their chances of finding her. "Within a couple of weeks, we knew she had been murdered, because we knew she would never leave her children. Her mom was devastated...her family was devastated."

Unfortunately, investigators were unable to find any clues to her whereabouts and admitted that they had no idea what had happened to her. John insisted he was innocent of any wrongdoing; detectives found no concrete evidence of foul play and John was never considered a suspect. A spokesperson for the Nassau County Police Department admitted that John hadn't gone out of his way to cooperate with them, and "did not grant permission to search any of the family properties and there was insufficient probable cause to obtain a warrant."

He told detectives that he believed Norine had been killed after a dispute in the Pathmark parking lot. "I think she was murdered. That's what I think, and we just haven't ever found her. There was a report that a lady seen an argument there." Investigators followed up on this report but were unable to confirm it. "At the time of the investigation, no other witnesses came forward to support this report, so it could not be verified nor could it be ruled out."

Aware that some people suspected him of doing something to his wife, John hired a lawyer and rarely spoke about the case publicly. He had Norine declared legally dead and cut off all ties with her family, denying them visitation with the couple's children. He later went on to get remarried and have two more children with his new wife.

The news media never paid much attention to Norine's case and it went cold almost immediately. Decades went by and her fate remained a mystery. In 2017, some of her old high school classmates started talking about her at their 40th reunion, and it upset them that she had never been found. Maria noted, "We said we have to reopen the case. Even if we don't find out what happened to her, just to find her and put her to rest and bring her home – that is what we want for her."

In 2019, Norine's friends received a tip that her body might have been disposed of in an old well located in the backyard of the apartment building where Norine and John had lived. They passed the information along to detectives, who confirmed that the well had been sealed off years earlier. A spokesperson for the Nassau County Police Department said that the well was considered a place of interest and they would be looking into it; it's unclear if it was ever searched.

John Brown continued to maintain his innocence and told reporters that detectives were welcome to ask him any questions they wanted. "I'm not stopping them from doing anything, I've never stopped them from anything...other than when they started getting crazy with me and my lawyer got involved."

As of December 2024, Norine's missing person case is still open. None of her loved ones believe that she is still alive, but they hope to find out what happened to her and would like to be able to give her a proper burial. Her friend Maria noted, "We owe it to Norine to keep trying. We are just hoping that someone has heard something that could lead us to what happened to her."

Norine Higuchi Brown was just 31 years old when she vanished from New Hyde Park, New York in December 1990. She was a devoted mother of two young children who had spent the day before she went missing getting ready for Christmas. Norine has brown eyes and brown hair, and at the time of her disappearance, she

was 5 feet 3 inches tall and weighed 120 pounds. She was last seen wearing red pants, a dark wool coat, and white sneakers. If you have any information about Norine's disappearance, please contact the Nassau County Police Department at 516-573-8800.

KELLIE BROWNLEE

Kellie Brownlee wanted to find a good summer job, and she wanted to make sure she found one before all the area college students started coming home for break. She told her boyfriend, Mark Graves, about the kind of job she wanted as they rode the bus to Walled Lake Western High School on the morning of May 20, 1982. Mark assured her she still had plenty of time, but she decided that she was going to skip class that day so she could go to the mall and fill out some job applications. She told Mark she would see him later that night, and walked away from the high school.

Although Kellie was 17 years old, she hadn't gotten her driver's license yet and her preferred mode of transportation was to hitchhike. She successfully hitched a ride, asking to be dropped off five miles away at the Twelve Oaks Mall in Novi, Michigan. Several people saw her at the mall, where she filled out applications at a few different fashion retailers.

Around 11:00 am, Kellie ran into Judy Mehay, the mother of one of her friends. She asked Kellie if she needed a ride back home, but Kellie told her she wanted to fill out a few more applications before she left the mall. Her friend's mother would be the last person known to see Kellie before she disappeared.

Kellie had been going through a bit of a rough time in the spring of 1982. Six weeks before she went missing, she had moved in with her boyfriend and his parents; although she loved her mother dearly, she didn't get along with her stepfather and had recently disclosed to friends that he had been abusing her.

Most people thought that Paul Brownlee was Kellie's father; she had always used his last name and very few people were aware of the fact that he was actually her stepfather. Kellie's mother, Loretta, had married Paul when she was very young and he had raised her and her older sister, Kim. From the outside, they appeared to be an ideal family; for Kellie and Kim, things were far from ideal.

In 1977, Kellie's older sister accused Paul of sexually abusing her. He eventually pleaded guilty to fourth degree criminal sexual misconduct; Kim moved to California to live with her biological father. Although Kellie had considered moving with her, she was extremely close to her mother and didn't want to leave her. She made the decision to stay in Michigan.

Although Kellie never told her friends why Kim had moved to California, many of them suspected that Paul was physically abusing Kellie. She often had bruises on her; friends had once counted Kellie's bruises and noted there were 32 of them. Though she was quiet about her homelife, over the next several years Kellie would occasionally leave home and stay with friends for a few weeks at a time when she was tired of dealing with Paul. She remained devoted to her mother, though, and was always in constant contact with her.

In April 1982, Kellie had once again decided that she couldn't live under the same roof with Paul. She moved away from her West Bloomfield, Michigan home and in with Mark in Walled Lake. Loretta desperately wanted her daughter to move back home, but Kellie held firm this time; she refused to return until her mother got rid of Paul. Loretta had given various reasons why she stayed with Paul over the years, but the main reason had always been financial. Now, she was almost finished with nursing school and knew that she would be able to support herself and her daughter without any help from Paul. It was simply a matter of time.

Kellie planned to return as soon as Paul was gone, and she believed that it would be soon. When she filled out all of her job applications that day, she listed the West Bloomfield address as her home address.

Mark wasn't too surprised when Kellie didn't return to school before classes were over for the day, but as the night wore on and there was still no sign of her, he began to worry. By 9:00 pm, he was extremely concerned and started calling around to Kellie's friends. He was hoping that she had simply run into someone she knew at the mall and had gone to their house, but no one he called had seen her at all that day.

By 11:00 pm, Mark had called everyone he could think of that might have seen Kellie, but none had been able to help him. As he discussed the situation with several of Kellie's close friends, they decided that they needed to call Loretta. Even when she wasn't living at home, Kellie always maintained close contact with her mother; her friends hoped that she had called her mother from the mall and had decided to go home with her for the night.

One of Kellie's closest friends, Carrie, offered to make the call. Her heart sank when Loretta answered the phone and told her that she hadn't heard from Kellie that day. Carrie wasn't really sure what to say, so she simply blurted out that Kellie appeared to be missing. Loretta's world changed in that moment. She immediately knew something had to be seriously wrong and called the police.

One of the first to be interviewed by detectives was Mark Graves. He told police that Kellie had skipped school that day, but only because she wanted to get a good summer job. He was certain she wouldn't have voluntarily run off; all of her belongings were still at home, and the only thing she had been carrying with her was her purse. Investigators searched through Mark's apartment, but found nothing to indicate that anything had happened to Kellie there and he was ruled out as a suspect early in their investigation.

Detectives were able to verify that Kellie had made it safely to the mall that morning, and witnesses had seen her there as late as 11:00 am. After that, it was unclear what had happened to her. They assumed she hadn't been abducted from the mall by a stranger, as it had been crowded with shoppers and someone likely would have witnessed something.

Investigators couldn't rule out the possibility that she left the mall with someone she knew; it was also possible that she ran into foul play after hitching a ride with the wrong person. Detectives, however, believed the answer might be closer to home. There was much speculation, by both law enforcement and Kellie's friends, that Paul Brownlee had done something to Kellie. He certainly had a motive; he was aware that she was pressuring her mother to divorce him and he knew that she had finally started telling people that he was abusing her. He had much to gain from her disappearance.

Paul claimed that he was nowhere near the mall during the time that Kellie was there and he insisted that he would never hurt her. He claimed that he spent the morning visiting his father-in-law's grave and had gone to work out at the gym after that. Detectives asked him if he would be willing to take a polygraph examination concerning Kellie's disappearance; he initially agreed, but then retained a lawyer and refused to cooperate any further.

Although detectives still considered Paul a person of interest, they had no evidence against him; not even the abuse allegations made by Kellie had been substantiated at the time of her disappearance. They were forced to place him on the back shelf of potential suspects and move on with their investigation.

While Kellie had a little bit of a wild streak, she was known as a genuinely nice teenager and had never been in any sort of criminal trouble. Like her friends, she preferred to wear tight jeans and army jackets, listen to heavy metal – she was in love with Ozzy Osbourne – and smoke Marlboro reds. They would sometimes skip school and hang out in a diner drinking coffee; they were also known to drink alcohol when they were able to get someone to buy it for them. Kellie told her mother that her motto was "live, love & laugh" and she certainly abided by it. She could also be very responsible and had no problem with the idea of working for a living. Although somewhat rebellious, with the exception of her habit of hitchhiking, Kellie wasn't living a very high-risk lifestyle.

Detectives followed up on all tips they received in the case, but were unable to develop any solid leads about where Kellie might have gone. Although most of those working on the case were convinced that Kellie had run into foul play, there were several reported sightings of her in the area. Investigators visited several different places where Kellie was said to have been seen, but were never able to confirm any of the sightings.

Although Paul still refused to sit down and be interviewed, he called detectives frequently with tips about potential sightings and possible theories. He also offered a $1,000 reward for information leading to her safe return. Some of the detectives were suspicious about the way he kept inserting himself into the investigation, but he still refused to be interviewed and there was little they could do. Slowly, the case started to stall and then went cold.

Loretta finally divorced Paul, but not until 1985. Even after the divorce, Paul continued to call detectives to offer tips about potential sightings of his ex-stepdaughter. In 1991, he showed up at the police station clutching a swimsuit catalog. He insisted that one of the models looked exactly like Kellie, and even provided police with a contact number for the person who hired the models for the catalog. Detectives believed he was simply trying to get them to update him on the state of the investigation; they pointed out that Kellie would be 26 in 1991 while the model he was showing them appeared to be about 12 years old.

Over the years, police have followed up on dozens of potential sightings of Kellie from all over the country. One tipster swore Kellie was playing the character of Snow White at Disneyland in California, another that she was a New York City topless dancer. Leads have come from New Mexico, Illinois, and Indiana; all of them led to dead ends. Despite this, authorities still believe that they will one day be able to solve the case and it is still considered an active investigation.

In 2018, police announced that they were looking into the possibility that Kellie might have been killed by suspected serial killer Arthur Ream. Currently serving a life sentence for the murder of Cindy Zarzycki, a Michigan girl who went missing in 1986, Ream had claimed that he killed others not yet found by police. Although so far detectives have found nothing to substantiate the theory that Ream was involved in Kellie's disappearance, they continue to pursue all leads.

Kellie Brownlee was 17 years old when she went missing in 1982. She has brown eyes and brown hair, and at the time of her disappearance she was 5 feet 7 inches tall and weighed 130 pounds. She was last seen wearing white pants, a long-sleeved peach blouse, and a pair of burgundy Nina-brand high-heels. She was carrying a wine-colored purse, and her ears were double-pierced but it is unknown if she was wearing earrings at the time. If you have any information about Kellie, please contact the West Bloomfield Police Department at 810-682-1563.

STEVEN CHAIT

Steven Chait left his dormitory at Columbia University around 3:30 pm on Monday, March 13, 1972. The 20-year-old didn't tell his roommate where he was going, and he didn't take any of his belongings with him when he left, leading his roommate to believe he would be back shortly. Yet Steven never returned to his room and was never seen again.

Steven's parents, Harry and Gloria Chait, lived in Flushing, New York. Steven's roommate called them two days after Steven went missing and let them know what was going on. His parents were immediately worried; Steven had never been the type of person to skip class, and he had also failed to show up for his scheduled shifts at Mama Joy's deli, where he worked part-time to help pay for his tuition.

After several days without any contact from Steven, Harry called the New York Police Department and reported him missing. Initially, however, police were unconcerned; they told the upset parents that Steven was an adult, free to come and go as he pleased. Investigators thought it was likely that Steven had simply been stressed about school and had decided to take some time to himself. They tried to assure Harry and Gloria that he would contact them when he was ready.

Steven was the oldest of Harry and Gloria's three children. He had always been highly intelligent; he learned to read at an early age and by the time he was in elementary school he was regularly reading newspapers and magazines geared toward adults. He wasn't just book smart; he was also a gifted athlete who had won awards for track when he was in high school.

When he learned that he had been accepted into Columbia University, Steven was thrilled. It was his dream school, and he was excited to start working toward a degree in engineering. Although his hometown of Flushing was only a half-hour drive from Columbia University, Steven opted to live on campus so he could have the full college experience. He moved into Furnald Hall and happily settled into life as a student at one of the country's most prestigious universities.

Everything went well during Steven's first year at Columbia, but during his second year, he had been horrified when he got a "C" in one of his engineering classes that was required for his major. For someone like Steven, who was used to excelling in school, it was a devastating blow. He had been so upset about his grade that he decided to take drastic action: he switched his major from engineering to art history.

Those close to Steven noticed a change in his behavior in the weeks leading up to his disappearance. His mother said he appeared to be "haunted by defeat." Gloria asked him a few times if he was doing okay, but he always avoided going into any detail about anything that might be bothering him. She last saw him the day before he went missing; he had come home to Flushing to spend the weekend with his parents. He left Sunday night to go back to his dormitory, then spent much of the next morning in his room listening to classical music.

Around 3:30 pm, Steven got up and turned his stereo off. He put on his jacket and hat, then wrapped a scarf around his neck. As he left the room, he glanced over at his roommate, waved slightly, and said, "Take it slow."

He then walked out the door, never to return.

Harry and Gloria did everything they could to persuade the New York Police Department to search for their son, but it soon became clear that they were not willing to invest any manpower into the case. They continued to insist that Steven had left on his own and would return soon. His parents pointed out that everything Steven owned – including his clothing, money, and passport, where left behind in his dorm room. If he just wanted to get away for a while, he likely would have taken at least a few things with him.

His parents feared that Steven had suffered some kind of mental breakdown and were desperate to find him before anything bad could happen to him. They scoured the city and beyond for any sign of Steven, paying special attention to places they knew their son liked to frequent. They were unable to find any trace of Steven.

Prior to his disappearance, Steven had a wide range of interests and took part in a number of activities on campus. He loved art, especially paintings, and he was a member of the New York Metropolitan Museum of Art and The National Gallery in Washington, D.C.; he also enjoyed spending time outdoors and was a member of the Sierra Club. He regularly donated blood to the American Red Cross. He was on Columbia University's track team and was in excellent physical health when he went missing.

On Mother's Day, the phone rang in the Chait's Flushing home. When Gloria answered it, she heard only silence and a faint crackle of static. The line didn't disconnect, and Gloria was sure that Steven was at the other end, wanting to let her know that he was alive but unwilling to speak. Certain her son could hear her, Gloria told him how much his parents loved him and pleaded with him to come home. After a few minutes, whoever was at the other end of the line hung up the phone without saying anything.

As weeks turned into months, Harry and Gloria grew increasingly worried about what had happened to their oldest son. They placed several ads in local papers, pleading for information about his whereabouts. The small classified ad featured a photograph of Steven and noted, "Desperately sought...any information will be deeply appreciated." The Chaits included their home phone number in the ad and prayed that someone would reach out to them with good news.

As the first anniversary of their son's disappearance approached, Harry and Gloria wrote a letter to a local newspaper, begging for help in finding Steven. They said that no one had heard a word from the college student since he left his dorm room a year earlier, and they just wanted to know that he was okay.

Harry and Gloria's grief was palpable. "We are two honest, hard-working people who have been reduced to despair by the disappearance of our first-born son...the complete silence has become unbearable...the shock of his leaving is still with us."

Steven's parents acknowledged that he might have felt the need to get away from his studies for a while, but they didn't believe he would have voluntarily stayed out of contact with them for so long. "We love our son deeply and it is our most fervent wish to reach out and to help him in his time of need...we know that we are capable of helping him if only we are given the opportunity."

For Harry and Gloria, life had become a nightmare. "Our peace of mind has been destroyed...we have been unable to establish the most vital and, at this time, the most haunting question for us, his parents: is he alive? We must know. Our lives are being destroyed. Please help us."

Despite the Chait's plea for help, Steven's disappearance soon faded from the minds of everyone except those who loved him. It failed to generate any media interest, and the fact that police had classified him as voluntarily missing didn't help. Harry and Gloria struggled to move on with their lives; Harry started drinking more, while Gloria found herself crying often. The silence in the home only increased when their second son, Gary, left for college.

Gary's departure from the home meant that the Chait's daughter, Risa, was the only child left to deal with her parents' depression. She was still in high school when her brother went missing, and she coped with the situation by spending much of her time with friends until she graduated from high school and enrolled in Yale. She later recalled that her parents had tried to play an active role in their remaining children's lives, but were often in their own little world. "They did the best they could for us, but they couldn't function."

Harry and Gloria found themselves isolated in their hometown, with many of their friends unsure of how to deal with their loss. Gloria noted, "People used to cringe when they saw me, like I was a witch." Perhaps because they were afraid of saying the wrong thing, people simply stopped saying anything to the couple. Their once vibrant social life faded away and they became even more isolated.

Eventually, Harry realized that something had to change. Steven was gone, but he knew that drinking every night wasn't going to bring him back so he swore off alcohol and tried to move on with his life. Gloria had a harder time; she wasn't willing to give up on her oldest son. She spent countless hours writing to anyone she thought might be able to help her and walked for miles along the city streets, searching for Steven among the homeless.

For the next 25 years, Gloria pinned her hopes on the fact that she continued to get mysterious phone calls; she was certain that it was Steven who was calling, though he never spoke a word. The calls would come a few times a year. Whenever Gloria would answer, there would be only silence, but her mother's intuition told her it was her son at the other end of the line. Although he never replied, she would speak to him, telling him over and over again how much his family loved him and wanted to see him again. After a minute or two, the line would disconnect, and Gloria would wait anxiously for the next call.

The phone calls stopped for good in 1997. Gloria never learned the identity of the mysterious caller but remained convinced that it had been Steven. If it had been him, she could only imagine why the calls suddenly stopped. Maybe he had finally moved on and no longer felt the need to hear his mother's voice. Perhaps he had died.

Harry died in 2002 after suffering a brain hemorrhage, leaving Gloria dealing with the grief of losing her husband as well as the loss of her oldest child. Several years later, she finally decided to go through Steven's old bedroom and get rid of his things. She donated some of his clothing, which had been hanging in his closet for more than three decades. In 2007, as the 35th anniversary of Steven's disappearance approached, she told a reporter that she was still determined to find him. "I'm never going to give up. He's too precious to me."

Steven Norman Chait was just 20 years old when he disappeared from Columbia University in New York

City in March 1972. An intelligent and socially conscious young man, Steven had initially hoped to become an engineer but gave up his dream after getting a 'C' in one of his classes. For someone used to excelling at everything he did, getting an average grade was unacceptable. It's unclear exactly what happened to Steven after he left his dorm room, but his mother received mysterious phone calls for the next 25 years and was convinced that it was her oldest son calling. Police had no evidence Steven was dead, so she might have been right. Steven has green eyes and brown hair, and at the time of his disappearance, he was 5 feet 10 inches tall and weighed 155 pounds. If you have any information about Steven, please contact the New York Police Department at 646-610-6914.

SHAWN DICKERSON

Shawn Dickerson left his San Francisco, California apartment shortly after 11:00 am on Friday, December 2, 2011. The 23-year-old was in a rush because he had overslept and was late for his job as a salesperson at Rolo, a men's clothing store in downtown San Francisco. Shawn had only been working at the store for about a month, and as he left the apartment he told one of his roommates that he needed to hurry so he could get there as soon as possible. He never arrived at work, however, and he didn't call his supervisor to say he wouldn't be in that day.

Instead of going to work, Shawn wandered around the city for hours, occasionally taking photographs with his iPhone. Shortly after 4:00 pm, he posted some of these photographs on Facebook, including one which showed his legs and feet, another featuring a plate of food at an unknown restaurant, and one of sand and water, presumably taken at San Francisco Bay. It's unclear what Shawn did after he posted the photographs. He never returned to his apartment and he was never seen again.

Shawn's roommates would later learn that Shawn had left his job early the day before; he arrived at work on time but failed to return to work after his lunch break. His boss sent him a text message asking him where he was, and Shawn didn't respond until 11:30 pm. He said he was sorry and blamed his early departure on the fact that he had autism. His boss hadn't been pleased and told Shawn that he wasn't going to have a job there for long if he continued to be so unreliable.

According to Shawn's mother, Tricia Brucker, Shawn had never been diagnosed with autism but friends and family thought it was possible he had either autism or Asperger's syndrome. He liked to spend time alone and tended to disconnect from society for days at a time. He rarely used his social media accounts and once got a new cell phone number without telling anyone, leaving them without a way of contacting him. It also appeared he didn't want people to easily find him on Facebook; shortly before he vanished, he changed his profile name on the site to Klaus Agnes.

Prior to his disappearance, Shawn spoke with his mother, who lived in Colorado, a few times a month. Although he hadn't seen her for around two years, he had been planning to visit her the following month. Tricia noted that he had seemed to be happier in recent months and had been looking forward to the future.

Shawn had been living in San Francisco for about six years. He had been born and raised in Ceres, California; except for a brief period when he lived in New York City, Shawn had always been a California boy. He rarely had a place of his own; during his time in San Francisco, he often stayed with friends. In August 2011, he moved into an apartment with five other people, one of whom was Anjuli Droll, a close friend he had dated during high school. The two of them planned to move to New York City once they had saved up some money.

Anjuli was the last person at the apartment to see Shawn before he disappeared; she watched him rush out the door saying he had to get to work. There had been nothing about his demeanor to suggest that anything was wrong, and she had no idea that he was going to ditch work and spend the day walking around San Francisco.

When Anjuli saw the pictures Shawn posted to his

Facebook page, she immediately knew where he was as she had been to those places with him. "When we weren't working, we would walk through Chinatown, up Columbus, and to the Aquatic Park and Fort Mason." She had no idea where he might have gone after he posted the pictures on Facebook.

Except for his phone and wallet, Shawn didn't take anything with him when he left the apartment that morning. Shawn always liked to dress nicely, but all of his shirts and pants were still hanging neatly in his closet. There was no note left behind, nothing to indicate that Shawn hadn't planned to come back to the apartment that afternoon.

At first, Shawn's friends and family members hoped that he had just decided to take a spontaneous trip somewhere and waited for him to show back up at the apartment with a good explanation for where he had been. As more time went by, however, they started to worry that something had happened to him and reported him missing to the San Francisco Police Department. Since he was an adult, however, police said he was free to come and go as he pleased. They did little to try and find him.

Shawn wasn't the first young man to go missing from San Francisco, and he wouldn't be the last. In a three-year period, a total of five men – including Shawn – were reported missing from the city and their families believe that their disappearances could be linked. San Francisco police deny this, but there are some similarities in each case.

Jackson Miller, a 19-year-old, was the first to go missing; he was last seen May 15, 2010, when he parked his car near the Golden Gate Bridge and walked away, leaving all of his personal belongings inside the vehicle. Surveillance cameras on the bridge filmed him as he walked away from the bridge's entrance and disappeared from view.

Jackson had suffered from depression and there was speculation he drove to the bridge with the intent to kill himself, but he never walked onto the bridge. Police watched all the surveillance footage from May 15th and May 16th and confirmed that there was no sign of Jackson. The weather had been clear and sunny on both days, so there were no areas of the bridge that were obscured from the surveillance cameras. Police admitted they had no idea where Jackson had gone after he walked away from his car.

According to Jackson's mother, there were at least four sightings of Jackson on May 19, 2010, four days after he left the bridge area. His family found the sightings convincing, leading them to believe that Jackson was still alive, but they were worried about his mental state. In addition to depression, he suffered from OCD. Like Shawn Dickerson, Jackson liked to dress neatly; his clothes were always perfect and he would usually use gel to style his hair exactly how he wanted it. It was hard to imagine him living on the streets, and his loved ones were desperate to find him. Sightings soon dried up, however, and his fate remained a mystery.

On October 6, 2011, two months before Shawn was last seen, 29-year-old Cameron Remmer vanished while he was staying at the Fairmount Hotel in San Francisco. Cameron had traveled to San Francisco on September 30, 2011, with $30,000 in cash he planned to use to buy marijuana so he could start a medical marijuana business.

Everything seemed to be going well until 11:00 pm on October 6, 2011, when Cameron called a friend in Arizona and said he needed someone to pay for his hotel room that night. His friend told him that he would pay, but Cameron then said not to worry about it because he had already found another place to stay. It's unknown where Cameron planned to stay that night; his friend in Arizona was the last person to speak with him before his cell phone went dead.

All of Cameron's belongings – including money and around 60 packages of marijuana – were left behind when he vanished. He had given them to the doorman at the Fairmount Hotel and told him that he would be back soon to pick them up.

Cameron had previously been diagnosed with bipolar disorder and had been hospitalized because of it at least once. He had also sustained several head injuries. It's unclear if these had anything to do with his disappearance, but like Jackson Remmer, there were repeated sightings of Cameron in the days after he walked away from the hotel. His loved ones feared that he was living on the streets, but they were unable to confirm any of the sightings. Exactly what happened to Cameron remained a mystery.

On February 7, 2013, 20-year-old Crishtian Hughes vanished while staying with a friend in San Francisco. He had flown to the city from San Diego earlier that week for a visit and was supposed to fly back home on the day he disappeared. According to his friend, Crishtian had gathered his belongings and left the house around 1:00 am, never to return. It's unclear where he planned on going; he didn't have a car in San Francisco and wasn't carrying much money.

In the months following his disappearance, there were several reported sightings of Crishtian in San Francisco, but none of them could be confirmed. Crishtian – and all of his belongings – seemed to vanish into thin air.

Sean Sidi, a 19-year-old who lived in San Francisco,

went missing on May 21, 2013, after stopping to visit with one of his former teachers at the French American International School. At 1:34 pm, he called his father and said he was heading to a nearby park, but when his father tried to call him about 30 minutes later, Sean didn't answer his phone. He was never heard from again.

About six months before he went missing, Sean had an accident in which he fell and crushed the right side of his skull. He was in a coma for several days and wasn't expected to survive, but managed to pull through. He suffered a traumatic brain injury, however, and had lasting side effects from the accident. His severe head injury left him medically fragile and he rarely ventured out alone.

Sean's last cell phone ping had come from the area near Golden Gate Park, Park Presidio, or Lands End; at 2:00 pm, his phone was either turned off or his battery died. His parents feared the worst when they couldn't get a hold of him and reported him missing to the San Francisco Police Department, stressing that his injury made him extremely vulnerable. His mother, Lynn Ching, noted, "If you or I get a bump on our heads, it's no big deal. But if he gets a bump on his head, the pressure could rise really fast and that would be dangerous. Because of the severity of his injury, he's much, much, much more vulnerable to complications that could be fatal."

Sean's friends and family organized several searches of the area surrounding Golden Gate Park. One woman told Lynn that she thought she had seen Sean on the day he went missing; he had indicated that he needed to cross over the Golden Gate Bridge and asked the woman for directions. Lynn went directly to the San Francisco police and asked them to review surveillance footage from the bridge and surrounding area to see if any of the cameras had captured Sean, but she said police refused to do so.

According to Lynn, police told her that there was no indication Sean met with foul play and they consider him to be voluntarily missing, despite the fact that he had been suffering from a traumatic brain injury. She pleaded with them to elevate his status to "endangered missing" so that other jurisdictions would know to keep an eye out for him, but they refused. Sean remained listed as voluntarily missing.

Doctors warned that Sean's head injury put him at risk of death if he wasn't found soon; hoping to bring in some new leads, his family announced that they were offering a $5,000 reward for information leading to his whereabouts. Although there were a few reported sightings of the missing man, none of them led the family to Sean.

On September 14, 2013, families of the five missing young men gathered together to hold a joint vigil in Golden Gate Park. Lynn said the families had decided to hold the vigil to raise awareness about the fact that Sean, Crishtian, Shawn, Cameron, and Jackson were still missing; they also wanted people to know how much trouble they had getting police to help them find their missing loved ones.

San Francisco Police Lt. Ed Santos wasn't convinced that the five cases were related. "I do not see a common link. There may be some cases where one might be similar to another, but when you really look at it, it's not."

Whether or not their cases are linked, the friends and family members of the five missing men share the same feelings of grief and uncertainty. All five cases have gone cold and are not being actively investigated by law enforcement. Loved ones don't know if the men are dead or simply lost to the streets of San Francisco, but they continue to hope that they will one day get answers about what happened to Jackson, Cameron, Shawn, Crishtian, and Sean.

Jackson Miller was 19 years old when he went missing on May 15, 2010. Jackson has blue eyes and brown hair, and at the time of his disappearance, he was 5 feet 11 inches tall and weighed 155 pounds.

Cameron Remmer was 29 years old when he went missing on October 6, 2011. Cameron has blue eyes and blond hair, and at the time of his disappearance, he was 5 feet 10 inches tall and weighed 170 pounds.

Shawn Dickerson was 23 years old when he went missing on December 2, 2011. Shawn has blue eyes and blond hair, and at the time of his disappearance, he was 5 feet 8 inches tall and weighed 140 pounds.

Crishtian Hughes was 20 years old when he went missing on February 7, 2013. Crishtian has hazel eyes and brown hair, and at the time of his disappearance, he was 5 feet 8 inches tall and weighed 140 pounds.

Sean Sidi was 19 years old when he went missing on May 21, 2013. Sean has brown eyes and brown hair, and at the time of his disappearance, he was 5 feet 5 inches tall and weighed 120 pounds.

All five men were last seen in San Francisco, California. If you have any information about Jackson, Cameron, Shawn, Crishtian, or Sean, please contact the San Francisco Police Department at 415-553-0123.

TIFFANY DIXON

Tiffany Dixon and her younger cousin, Israel Morales, left their Brooklyn, New York home around 7:00 am on Thursday, October 10, 1991. Tiffany accompanied 8-year-old Israel to a nearby bus stop, where they got on the first of two buses they would take each morning. The second bus dropped them off near Carroll Elementary School, where Israel was a third-grade student. Tiffany made sure Israel got to his classroom safely, then began walking in the direction of her junior high school, which was located four blocks away from the elementary school. The 12-year-old never made it to her school that day, and she was never seen again.

Tiffany lived with her aunt, Norma Delgado, in Brooklyn's Bushwick neighborhood. Norma started to worry when the seventh-grader failed to come home from school Thursday afternoon; Israel was escorted home by a classmate's parent. Her concern grew when she learned that Tiffany hadn't attended any of her classes that day. She called the New York Police Department and reported her niece missing.

Initially, police didn't seem too concerned about Tiffany's disappearance. They seemed to think she was a runaway and would return home within a few days. It wasn't until the following week that the 83rd Precinct Detective Squad issued a missing person alert with Tiffany's description and asked the public to keep an eye out for her.

Norma told reporters that she was certain Tiffany

had not run away from home. She was an excellent student who had recently been accepted into a magnet program at her junior high; she was taking high-level math and science classes and seemed to thoroughly enjoy the work. Friends described her as a "homework freak" who liked to spend much of her free time in the school's library. She often said that she wanted to be a scientist when she was older, and her teachers believed she had the talent to do so.

Tiffany's biological mother, Iris Franco, had been unable to take care of her after she got divorced seven years earlier; Iris had asked her sister, Norma, to take over guardianship of Tiffany. Norma, who had two children of her own, treated Tiffany as if she were her daughter. "Anybody who knows me knows I have three children. Israel, Miguel, and Tiffany. They're her brothers."

Tiffany had always been an extremely reliable child; she never skipped class and was always on time to pick Israel up after school each afternoon. The elementary school principal, Linda Leff, noted, "She was always very concerned about her brother. She was very responsible about him." She got along well with her classmates and never got into any trouble at school. "She was a happy, smiling child. She never seemed to have any problems."

Walter Sadowski, the principal of Tiffany's junior high school, told reporters that the four-block walk between the two schools was highly-trafficked and generally considered to be quite safe. "At that time of day, the streets are filled with people walking to the F train station on Smith Street." He couldn't imagine how something could have happened to Tiffany without anyone seeing anything.

Tiffany's disappearance worried parents throughout the school district. Camille Limardi, whose son was in Israel's class, noted, "I've never heard of anything like this happening in this neighborhood, and I've been here for 39 years." Susanne Gonsalves, who was also the mother of a third grader, told reporters, "It's a shock, a real shock...this isn't the kind of neighborhood where people would see something happen to a child and just let it happen."

Tiffany's family distributed missing person flyers throughout their Brooklyn neighborhood, but investigators received few tips in the case. On Saturday, November 2, 1991, around 150 volunteers took part in a search of the Carroll Gardens neighborhood where Tiffany was last seen. Norma, who organized the search, told reporters, "I've been going crazy. We'll hand out flyers and look around empty lots. The police are doing all they can, but it's not enough. My daughter is not home."

New York Detective Gerald Petillo said that investigators had followed up on each tip they received, but had been unable to develop any substantial leads and had no idea what had happened to Tiffany. "We have an unexplained disappearance of a 12-year-old girl. No one saw the girl being abducted off the street." Although they hadn't found any evidence of foul play, Detective Petillo noted, "We still have a few more avenues we have to investigate."

Weeks went by and Tiffany remained missing. Norma dreaded the thought of having to go through the Christmas season without Tiffany. "Last year she helped me carry the tree home and decorate." She was praying that Tiffany would be home before the holidays. "It has been two months, but you can't give up hope. If something bad had happened we would have known by now."

Two months after Tiffany was last seen, her

biological mother was admitted to Bellevue Hospital for the last time. She had been diagnosed with AIDS a couple of years earlier, and the disease took her life in December 1991. Norma went to visit her before she died. "The last words she said to me were, 'Please find my daughter.'"

Shortly before she went missing, Tiffany had told Norma that she wanted a leather jacket for Christmas. "I told her I would buy her the jacket if she was a good girl, but I never had to worry about her – she was always good." Norma bought the jacket and wrapped it up so she could put it under the Christmas tree in the hopes that Tiffany would be home to open it.

Norma's two sons were having trouble dealing with Tiffany's disappearance. Miguel, who was just five, missed Tiffany but didn't fully understand the situation. "Sometimes when I am sitting here alone and thinking about her, I cry. That's when Mikey comes up to me and hugs me and says, 'Mommy, don't worry. Tiffany will come home.'"

Israel seemed to be having the most difficulty adjusting to life without his older sister. "Every day she took him to school on two buses. He can't figure out why she is not here, and at night he cries himself to sleep." Norma noted that Tiffany had been extremely close with Israel, and she never would have willingly left him at school without anyone to escort him home.

As the holidays approached, Norma grew even more worried about Tiffany. "It is so cold out, and all she had on was a sweater. I pray for the best...I hope she comes home for Christmas."

Tiffany didn't make it home for Christmas that year, and the investigation into her disappearance soon went cold. Detectives were unable to find anyone who recalled seeing the 12-year-old after she dropped Israel off at his classroom and headed down the tree-lined street toward her junior high school.

Years went by, and Tiffany's family continued to hold out hope that she would one day be returned to them. Every Christmas, Norma would hang Tiffany's stocking up along with the ones belonging to Israel and Miguel, and each year both boys prayed that Santa would bring their older sister back to them.

In 1999, Norma told reporters that she was always careful to use the present tense when she was speaking about Tiffany. "That she's dead – that's not a thought I'd even entertain."

The New York Police Department considers Tiffany to be an endangered missing person, but they still have no idea if she ran away from home or was a victim of foul play. Although the investigation into her disappearance remains open, there have been no new leads in decades and the case has been cold for almost as long as Tiffany has been missing.

Tiffany Madia Dixon was just 12 years old when she went missing from Brooklyn, New York in October 1991. She was an intelligent girl who hoped to be a scientist when she got older, and she had a very close relationship with her aunt, who she lived with, and her two younger cousins, who treated her as their sister. Tiffany has brown eyes and black hair, and at the time of her disappearance, she was 4 feet 11 inches tall and weighed 105 pounds. She was last seen wearing baggy blue pants, a white blouse, a black sweater, and black Nike sneakers. If you have any information about Tiffany, please contact the New York Police Department at 646-610-6914.

ROGER ELLISON

Roger Ellison woke up early on the morning of Tuesday, February 10, 1981, and got himself ready for school. The 17-year-old, a senior at Cedaredge High School in Cedaredge, Colorado, rode the bus to school as usual, arriving in plenty of time to go to his locker before he had to head to his homeroom. Roger spoke briefly to one of his friends as he grabbed the books he needed for his first period class, but what happened to him after that is a mystery. He didn't attend any of his classes that day and he was never seen again.

Roger's parents, Ernest and Evelyn Ellison, grew concerned when he didn't come home when school let out that afternoon. Roger, the youngest of their five children, was a dependable teenager who had no history of running away from home. He was a straight-A student and was looking forward to his high school graduation in a few months; he had been accepted at Western State College in Gunnison, Colorado, and had already picked out and paid for his dormitory room. He had no reason to disappear.

When they called Cedaredge High School, Roger's parents were surprised to learn that he had missed all of his classes that day. He wasn't the type of teenager anyone expected to skip school; prior to this, he had perfect attendance. Evelyn started calling all of her son's friends, but none of them had any idea where he could be. The couple spent a sleepless night waiting by the phone for a call that never came.

Early Wednesday morning, Roger's parents called

the Delta County Sheriff's Department and tried to report their son missing, but the sheriff said Roger hadn't been missing long enough. According to Evelyn, "He told us we had to wait 48 hours before he could begin a search." Unwilling to wait, the couple started driving around the area, searching in vain for any sign of Roger. "Suddenly, I was living every mother's nightmare."

On Friday, Roger's case was assigned to Delta County Detective Keith Waibel. Although he initially thought he was dealing with a juvenile runaway, he quickly realized that Roger wasn't the type of teenager one would expect to voluntarily vanish. He was a model student and a skilled skier who hoped to one day compete in the Olympics.

According to Roger's parents, the teen had taken part in a skiing competition in Telluride, Colorado the weekend before he went missing; he hoped he would score high enough to earn a spot on the US ski team but fell a little short. Although he had been disappointed with the results, he didn't seem overly depressed and was convinced he would do better when he competed in Aspen the following weekend.

He had been in a good mood before he left to go to school that morning. When he came into the kitchen for breakfast, he glanced out the window and told his mother that it looked like it might snow later that day. He commented that fresh snow would be a good omen for his upcoming ski competition, indicating that he had already moved on from his loss in Telluride.

Classmates described Roger as somewhat of a loner; his main interest was skiing and he didn't socialize as much as some teenagers. While he was always friendly to everyone, he was also quite shy and didn't go out of his way to be noticed. He had a close relationship with both of his parents, especially his father, who had been forced to retire early after a stroke and open heart surgery. The two of them spent a lot of time together.

Despite the fact that no one who knew Roger believed he had run away from home, Detective Waibel told reporters that he suspected Roger had gone to a ski resort in search of a job. Evelyn was certain this was not the case. "He always called when he would be late or left a note if he was leaving for someplace and we weren't home." She was sure he wouldn't have left home without warning.

Roger should have been celebrating his 18th birthday on March 11, 1981; his parents noted that since he was legally an adult, there would be no reason for him not to contact them as they couldn't make him come home if he didn't want to. Although they hoped they would hear from him once his birthday arrived, they weren't surprised when he failed to contact them. For them, it was just more proof that something bad had happened to him.

In May 1981, Roger's classmates gathered on the school's football field for their graduation. Ernest and Evelyn were too upset to sit in the stands and watch as one of Roger's friends accepted his diploma for him; instead, the couple sat in the car in the parking lot and cried.

By July, his parents were desperate to know what happened to him; hoping to bring in some new leads, they announced that they were offering an $8,000 reward for information leading to Roger's whereabouts. Evelyn wasn't sure her son was still alive. "We think there was foul play. He would've let us know by now. Maybe somebody's holding him or he saw something in Telluride that he wasn't supposed to see."

Detective Waibel admitted that he still had no idea where Roger might be but he didn't think foul play was involved. "I think he's out of the state. I think he just got fed up and left...I can't find any indication of foul play."

Roger's parents pointed out that he hadn't taken anything with him when he left for school that day; he had left with the clothes on his back and $3.00 in his wallet. All of his ski equipment was left behind, and his savings account, which contained $1,000 he planned to use to get a car or motorcycle, hadn't been touched. If he planned to run away to a ski lodge as Detective Waibel thought, he would have at least taken his skis. Evelyn ruefully noted, "He was such a good boy. He wasn't a runaway. But how do you convince people?"

Ernest told reporters that the uncertainty about his son's fate was extremely hard for him to handle. "It's awful not knowing. We've had deaths in the family. My wife and I both lost our parents. This is worse than that...we've spent a lot of money and heartbreak trying to locate our son...we have to keep going, but it doesn't look very good."

Sadly, Ernest would never learn what happened to his son. His health declined rapidly after Roger's disappearance, causing him to suffer from another stroke. He died on August 21, 1981, at the age of 58. Evelyn vowed to continue the search without him, supported by Roger's sister and three brothers.

In May 1982, Detective Waibel admitted that the case was a baffling one. "It looks like Roger Ellison just disappeared into thin air, but I know that can't happen. We've never had a single solid lead. We can't find a trace of where he went. This case has turned me into a blithering idiot."

Detective Waibel said he had gradually come to the

conclusion that Roger's parents were right; the teenager likely hadn't left voluntarily. "There was absolutely no evidence of a drug problem, no hint of mental illness, nothing to indicate Roger had been the slightest bit depressed."

Evelyn was willing to do anything to learn what had happened to her youngest son, but she admitted that she was overwhelmed with calls from "self-proclaimed psychics, amateur detectives, and a lot of weird people." She hired a private detective; though he readily took her money, he was unable to provide any information about Roger.

Evelyn struggled to stay positive. "You think nothing like this could ever happen to you. When it does, at first you can't believe it. But slowly you just sink into this depression, where you exist one day at a time, hoping that tomorrow, at last, you'll know what happened to your child."

Years went by without any progress on the case. In 1989, Delta County Sheriff Bill Blair, who had been a detective when Roger first went missing, admitted that the case was a complete mystery. "We have followed lead after lead after lead, but nothing has panned out. It's real tragic that we can't come up with something." He believed Roger met with foul play but lacked the evidence to prove it. "I have this little thing in my stomach that says he didn't get out of Cedaredge."

Like Sheriff Blair, Evelyn believed her son was likely somewhere close to home. She worried that he had been killed and dumped in an empty mine but lacked the resources needed to launch an extensive search. Sadly, like Ernest, Evelyn would never get the answers she wanted. She died at the age of 70 on February 9, 1992, one day shy of the 11th anniversary of Roger's disappearance.

In March 1994, Delta County detectives, along with a team from NecroSearch, dug up a large portion of a yard belonging to the Taylor Mortuary, located next to Cedaredge High School. Sheriff Blair said a recent tip from one of Roger's classmates led to the dig; at the time of Roger's disappearance, the property had been a private home belonging to John Pash, one of Roger's teachers.

John Pash taught psychology at Cedaredge High School; he also served as the school's wrestling coach. Evelyn had been somewhat suspicious of him from the start, noting that shortly after Roger vanished, John came to visit her and Ernest and told them that Roger had been suicidal and likely killed himself. This opinion wasn't shared by any of John's other teachers, all of whom said he was a pleasant and happy teenager who never exhibited any signs of depression.

John Pash claimed that he knew more about Roger than anyone else because he had been counseling Roger at his home. Evelyn told detectives she believed this was a lie, as Roger had often expressed that he didn't like John Pash, who made him stop by his home to drop off homework on at least one occasion. She was certain there was no way he would have agreed to be counseled by him, especially without telling his parents.

Witnesses said that shortly before Evelyn died, she reiterated her suspicions about John, telling people she always had a funny feeling he had been involved in her son's disappearance. She also believed that some of Roger's classmates likely knew more than they were admitting. Detectives agreed that it was time to start reinterviewing some of Roger's old friends and classmates, which led to the tip about the former Pash property.

John Pash had moved to California several years after Roger disappeared. While detectives declined to name him a suspect in the case, they returned to his former property in April 1994 and used ground-penetrating radar to look for potential gravesites. They identified a total of six anomalies, including two under concrete.

Investigators dug up four of the anomalies but found nothing; officials said more investigative work would have to be done before they could search the areas concealed by concrete. Sheriff Blair stated, "We need to do more interviewing and go another direction before digging up the whole countryside." Eventually, they dug up most of the yard; they found a bone they thought was human, but it turned out to be from an animal.

There was little movement on the case over the next few years. In 1998, Sheriff Blair told reporters he was certain there were people in Cedaredge who knew exactly what happened to Roger, but he questioned if the case would ever be solved. "We don't have a body, and even if we found one, we would have to have someone involved say, 'This is what happened.'"

In September 1998, Delta County Detective Dave Duncan received a call from a man who claimed to know what happened to Roger. The man, who was on his deathbed, said he wanted to clear his conscience before he died. According to Detective Duncan, the man and a friend were in the Cedaredge area poaching deer in early 1981 when they saw a young man they believed to be Roger being held at gunpoint by another man.

The dying man's friend came forward and corroborated the story. Both men said Roger told them the man was going to kill him. "Supposedly it was over a bad cocaine deal...Roger had absconded with the money and given it to friends." As the witnesses left the area, they heard two gunshots and assumed Roger had been killed. The dying man was given a polygraph examination about his account and he passed.

Investigators flooded the woods where the men claimed Roger had been shot, scouring the area for any sign of bones or bullets. They didn't find anything, but admitted that the lack of evidence didn't necessarily mean that the witnesses were lying, as any skeletal remains that hadn't been buried could have been spread out by scavengers years earlier.

No one close to Roger ever knew him to associate with drug users, but his brother, Roy, admitted that Roger had been acting strange the last time he saw him. Perhaps he had gotten involved in something that spiraled out of control and led to his death. The truth may never be known; more than four decades after Roger walked away from his locker and vanished, his fate remains a mystery.

Roger John Ellison was just 17 years old when he vanished from Cedaredge, Colorado in February 1981. A talented skier, Roger hoped to one day make it to the Olympics and was supposed to compete in a ski event the weekend after he vanished. Those close to Roger say he didn't drink or use drugs, but after he went missing there were rumors that drugs were somehow involved in his disappearance. While detectives were never able to find any proof of foul play, they don't believe that Roger voluntarily left. Roger has blue eyes and blond hair, and at the time of his disappearance, he was 6 feet tall and weighed 145 pounds. Roger was last seen wearing brown pants, a blue T-shirt, a light blue nylon jacket, white socks, and sneakers. If you have any information about Roger, please contact the Delta County Sheriff's Department at 970-874-9734.

MARGARET FOX

Margaret Fox was hoping to earn some extra money during the summer of 1974, so the 14-year-old placed an advertisement in a local newspaper stating that she was looking for babysitting work. On the morning of Monday, June 24, 1974, Margaret left her Burlington City, New Jersey home and took the bus to Mount Holly, where she was supposed to meet a potential client named John Marshall. She never returned home and she was never seen again.

Margaret and her cousin, 11-year-old Lynne Park, had gone together to place the babysitting advertisement in the local paper. The ad, which ran on Tuesday, June 18, 1974, included both of their phone numbers. John Marshall called Lynne on Wednesday and asked her if she could babysit his 5-year-old son, but Lynne's mother wouldn't allow her to do so as she thought it was too far from their home.

John Marshall called Margaret next and asked her if she were available; after checking with her parents, she said she would be able to babysit his son that Friday. Later that night, the man called the Fox home and spoke to her father, David Fox; he said he needed to move the babysitting job to Monday morning. David told investigators that the man sounded middle-aged, perhaps 35 to 45 years old. He said that his wife would pick up Margaret at the bus stop and would drive her home when she finished babysitting around 2:30 pm.

Margaret's 11-year-old brother, Joseph, walked to

the bus stop with her on Monday morning and waited with her until the bus arrived at 8:40 am. A passenger on the bus told detectives that she recalled seeing the teenager on the bus that morning, and another witness saw Margaret near the intersection where she had agreed to meet John Marshall's wife. No one saw her talking to anyone or getting into a vehicle after she got off the bus.

When Margaret failed to return home Monday afternoon, her parents started to worry about her. Unfortunately, Margaret hadn't gotten an address for John Marshall; he had told her only that his wife would meet her at the bus stop in a red Volkswagen. She did have a phone number he had given her, but when one of her parents called this number it turned out to be for a pay phone outside the A&P grocery store on Route 38 in Mount Holly.

Margaret's mother, Mary Jane Fox, started going through the phone book and calling every Marshall listed in Mount Holly. None of them had hired Margaret to babysit for them. With no way to reach John Marshall, David spent a couple of hours driving around Mount Holly, searching in vain for his daughter. As darkness fell without any sign of her, he returned home and called the Burlington City Police Department to report Margaret missing.

Burlington City Detective Raymond Butterfield said that Margaret had recently finished eighth grade at St. Paul's Grammar School in the city; she was a good student and got along well with her parents and siblings. She had no history of running away from home, and Det. Butterfield didn't believe she left on her own. He noted that the circumstances surrounding her disappearance were suspicious. "It doesn't look too right."

When Mount Holly Police Lt. Benjamin English was

told that detectives were looking for someone named John Marshall, he immediately pointed them in the direction of Jack Marshall, an old friend who was the assistant manager of the same A & P supermarket where the payphone was located. Lt. English noted, "I've known him for 25 years. He's the father of five grown children. I'm sure he's not involved."

Several detectives interviewed Jack Marshall but were unable to connect him to Margaret. On June 27, 1974, two FBI agents arrived at the A & P and questioned Jack; they seemed satisfied that he had no involvement in Margaret's disappearance. Jack himself appeared to be stunned by the situation. "I have no idea what is happening. I didn't even know the phone number outside had been used until this morning. I have no ideas, no theories...it's causing me a lot of trouble."

Detectives soon confirmed that Jack had an iron-clad alibi for the day of Margaret's disappearance; he also voluntarily took and passed a polygraph examination. Investigators were confident he hadn't been involved; the use of his name was deemed to be a coincidence.

Investigators spoke with all of Margaret's family members and many of her friends but were unable to find any reason why the teenager would have voluntarily vanished. Burlington Police Detective Leonard Burr admitted, "A lot of 14-year-old girls run away from home, but this is not the normal runaway pattern. I've spoken with her family and friends. They said she was very happy and had no reason to run away."

Margaret had five brothers; she was the only girl in the family and had no problems at home. Mary Jane noted, "She had no boyfriends, she hadn't started to date yet. She was never in trouble for anything." Her father described her as a homebody; she preferred to stick close to home but had decided to advertise her babysitting services so she could earn some extra spending money before she started high school in the fall.

After speaking with everyone who had known Margaret, officials were convinced that foul play was involved in her disappearance. They thought it was possible that the teenager's abductor might call the family looking for a ransom, so the FBI began recording all calls made to the Fox home. Four days after Margaret went missing, they got a call from an unidentified male. "$10,000 might be a lot of bread, but your daughter's life is the buttered topping."

The caller hung up before Margaret's parents could get any additional information from him, and it's still unknown whether he had anything to do with her disappearance or was simply someone looking to take advantage of her family.

The strange ransom call was followed up with several letters, each demanding $10,000. One letter noted, "Margaret is alright. We only tore her blouse and broke her glasses." Oddly, one of the letters mentioned the Symbionese Liberation Army. Detectives believed that the letters were likely a hoax but were never able to determine who sent them.

Over the next week, police were flooded with calls from people who believed they had seen Margaret, as well as from callers who thought they knew who was responsible for abducting the teenager. A few girls called to report bad experiences they had in the past when they advertised their babysitting services. Detectives followed up on each tip they received, but none of them brought them any closer to Margaret.

Burlington Police Chief George Clayton told reporters that they were still in the early stages of the investigation and weren't sure exactly what had happened to Margaret. He admitted that they only knew three things for certain: Margaret had advertised for a babysitting job, she received a phone call from someone claiming to be named John Marshall, and she boarded a bus headed for Mount Holly.

Chief Clayton told reporters that advertising services in the paper could be dangerous. "Anytime you put your telephone number or address in the newspaper, you are subject to any nut who wants to call you seeming to be legitimate." As word spread about Margaret's disappearance, investigators heard from dozens of parents who believed someone had tried to lure their daughters on false babysitting jobs; many now wondered if their daughter would have ended up missing or dead if they had been allowed to take the job offer.

In August 1974, police started receiving complaints that a man claiming to be a professional photographer for a modeling school had called a number of households in the area looking for models. He often identified himself as Bob Williams and said he worked for the Anderson Charm and Modeling School; no one at the school had ever heard of the man and confirmed that he was not on staff there.

Ernest Barratt of Rancocas, New Jersey, had been at home when his wife received a call from Bob Williams. He offered her a modeling job over the phone, but Ernest was suspicious and began questioning the man about his credentials. Ernest grew angry when the man kept asking for his wife's measurements; realizing he was getting nowhere, Bob Williams hung up. Ernest called police and said, "He definitely didn't sound professional. He used bad grammar and his phrasing was poor."

It was unclear if "Bob Williams" was the same one who had called Margaret, but detectives believed he might have been. Each of the women called by Bob Williams had recently had their names published in the local paper; one had been listed as an honor roll student, others were mentioned in editorials or in a family member's obituary.

By September, the phony modeling calls had stopped and little progress had been made on Margaret's case. As the three-month anniversary of her disappearance approached, her parents struggled to remain optimistic. Although they had initially hoped to find their daughter alive, both admitted that they feared she had been killed. Crying, David told a reporter that he just wanted to find her body. "At least she should have a decent burial."

Margaret's disappearance devastated her family. David tried not to think about it as he went to work each day, while Mary Jane found herself crying all the time. Joseph, the brother who had accompanied her to the bus stop the morning she went missing was overcome with feelings of guilt, wishing that he had done something to prevent her from getting on the bus. He had trouble sleeping and kept the light on in his bedroom all night. Princess, the family dog, was also hit hard by the loss of Margaret. She had always slept in Margaret's bed with her, now she moped around the house and refused to go upstairs near any of the bedrooms.

Hoping to bring in some new clues about their daughter's disappearance, David and Mary Jane offered a $2,000 reward for information leading to Margaret's recovery. Detectives continued to receive tips concerning possible sightings of the missing teenager, but they were unable to confirm any of them and didn't believe that Margaret was still alive.

By November 1975, Margaret had been missing for 17 months and her fate remained a mystery. David admitted to reporters that he didn't expect to see his daughter again, but tried to remain optimistic. "Some people feel it's hopeless. Sometimes, I just accept that. I think that it's over and done. But then sometimes I get this feeling that she's alive, that she's out there."

Detective Burr noted, "It's one of the most frustrating cases I've been involved in. The case is still open...we check everything out, but we just don't have anything." Investigators from Burlington City and Mount Holly, as well as the New Jersey State Police and the FBI, were continuing to do everything they could to find Margaret but kept hitting dead ends.

In January 1976, there were rumors about a potential break in the case. Officials admitted that a prison inmate in Pennsylvania had recently confessed to abducting and murdering Margaret, but after a thorough investigation detectives were confident that the man had nothing to do with the case. He had been in a hospital at the time Margaret disappeared and later admitted he had falsely confessed. The man, who was homeless, claimed he was hoping to be sentenced to life behind bars so he would be clothed, housed, and fed. Instead, he was sentenced to up to three years in prison for providing false information to police.

Decades passed and Margaret's case languished on the cold case shelf. Detectives continued to review her case file from time to time, but were never able to come up with any solid evidence of what happened to her. In 2001, Burlington Police Detective Sgt. John Stefanoni told reporters, "I grew up with Margaret, knew the family. The family was and still is a genuine American family. The father was the town plumber. They were devoted Catholics. I just can't imagine the tragedy this has put the family through."

In June 2019, the FBI offered a $25,000 reward for information leading to the person responsible for Margaret's disappearance. They also released a recording of the ransom call received by Margaret's parents four days after she went missing; it can be heard here: https://www.fbi.gov/audio-repository/newark-margaret-ellen-fox-phone-call-062419.mp3/view. They hoped that someone would recognize the voice of the man who made the call, but as of this writing, the caller remains unidentified.

Burlington City Police Chief John Fine admitted that Margaret was likely dead, but said the department was still committed to finding her. "It is our mission that if this is the case, Margaret receives a proper burial. The Fox family can have closure, receive the answers they deserve, and our community can begin to heal."

Margaret Ellen Fox was just 14 years old when she was last seen in Burlington City, New Jersey in June 1974. A friendly and intelligent girl who loved horses, Margaret hoped to earn some extra spending money by advertising her babysitting services in a local paper. She was excited when she received a call about her first job, but she never returned from a meeting with her client and detectives believe the job was a hoax. Margaret has blue eyes and brown hair, and at the time of her disappearance, she was 5 feet 2 inches tall and weighed 105 pounds. She was last seen wearing a blue flowered blouse, a blue and white checkered jacket, maroon flared jeans with a yellow patch on one knee, and brown sandals. She was also wearing a gold charm bracelet and a gold necklace with flowers and a blue stone. Margaret had freckles on her face and wore eyeglasses; she was missing two of her top teeth at the time of her disappearance. If you have any information about Margaret, please contact the Burlington City Police Department at 609-386-0262, extension 211, or the FBI's Newark Office at 973-792-3000.

ALI GILMORE

Ali Gilmore was expecting her first child and was extremely excited about becoming a mother. Thursday, February 2, 2006, was a normal day for the 30-year-old. She arrived at the Florida Department of Health office in Tallahassee, where she worked as a statistical analyst, promptly at 8:00 am. She left there around 5:00 pm and headed for her second job at a nearby Publix bakery. She finished her shift at 11:00 pm and told some of her coworkers that she planned to head straight home. They watched as she headed out into the parking lot carrying two slices of pizza she had purchased on her break; it would be the last time they ever saw her.

Ali grew up near West Palm Beach, Florida, and attended Jupiter High School. After her graduation in 1993, she moved to Tallahassee to attend Florida A & M University. When she graduated with a degree in health information management, she decided to remain in Tallahassee, drawn by the city's low crime rate and slower pace of life as compared to West Palm Beach. She was hired by the Florida Department of Health, where she quickly earned a reputation as a competent and compassionate employee.

Throughout high school and college, Ali had worked for the supermarket chain Publix, and she opted to stay there part-time even after taking a job with the Department of Health. It didn't leave her with a lot of free time, but Ali didn't seem to mind the long hours.

A year after she graduated from FAMU, Ali went to

a picture frame store in Tallahassee's Governor's Square Mall to buy a frame for her diploma. She immediately hit it off with the employee who waited on her, a man named James Gilmore. The attraction was mutual, and the two were soon dating. In October 2000, they got married.

James would later credit Ali for encouraging him to go back to school; he enrolled in Flagler College to study business when he was 29 years old. While the couple appeared to have a solid relationship, there was some stress in the marriage. Money was tight, as James had to pay child support for his three children from a previous relationship. To make ends meet, Ali had to continue working two jobs while James went back to school.

A couple of years after they got married, James and Ali purchased their first home together, a newly-constructed rancher in Tallahassee's Wilson Green subdivision. Between James attending college and Ali working two jobs, they rarely got to spend time together and the strain eventually became too much for their marriage. In the fall of 2005, the couple separated and James moved in with his brother.

A month or so after James had moved out, Ali learned that she was pregnant. She had always wanted children and was thrilled with the news, but she was cautious. She had gotten pregnant the previous year but had suffered a miscarriage, so she was careful not to do anything that might jeopardize her unborn child. She made sure she never attempted to lift anything heavy and even avoided climbing stairs when possible. Although she hadn't yet learned the sex of the baby, she was convinced she was having a girl and told friends she had been thinking about naming her Jasmine or Angel.

Although James and Ali had separated, they were committed to finding a way to make their relationship work. They started attending marriage counseling, and Ali told her coworkers she was hopeful that the two of them would be able to work through their differences and move forward as husband and wife.

Ali and James were scheduled to attend a counseling session on the morning of Friday, February 3, 2006, but James overslept and missed the appointment. He tried to call Ali at her office that afternoon to apologize but was surprised to learn that she had never shown up for work. Her colleagues agreed that it wasn't like her to miss a day without calling, but they weren't overly concerned. They knew she was pregnant and it was possible she might have had a doctor's visit that she had forgotten to mention.

James tried to call Ali a couple of times on Saturday but was unable to reach her. Thinking she might have been angry with him for missing their counseling session, he decided to give her some time to cool off.

When Ali failed to show up at work on Monday morning, her coworkers began to worry that something had happened to her. They waited until the end of the day, and when they still hadn't heard from Ali two of her coworkers drove to her house to see if she was there. Her car was in the driveway and her porch light was turned on, but no one answered the door when they knocked. At 8:00 pm Monday, Ali's supervisor called the Tallahassee police and asked them to do a welfare check on her missing employee.

Officers were dispatched to Ali's Loraine Court home. The house was locked and there were no signs of forced entry. They contacted James as well as some of Ali's neighbors, and all of them agreed that it would be completely out of character for her to go anywhere without letting someone know.

Police searched Ali's home but found nothing out of place. There was nothing to indicate that any sort of struggle had taken place inside the house or in Ali's car; only Ali and her house keys were unaccounted for. Still, the fact that Ali was four months pregnant and rarely out of contact with friends and family concerned police, and on Tuesday they had a forensic team comb through the house for clues to her whereabouts. They also impounded her car and processed it for possible forensic evidence. Nothing was found to suggest that foul play had taken place.

The subdivision where Ali lived was still under construction, and there were many partially constructed homes and vacant buildings. More than two dozen police officers carefully combed through the area looking for any sign of the missing woman, but came up empty. Detectives canvassed the neighborhood, questioning residents and learning more about Ali's daily habits. Everything they heard indicated that Ali had not gone missing voluntarily.

Investigators interviewed Ali's family, friends, and coworkers and determined that no one had any contact with her after she left Publix at 11:00 pm Thursday. It seemed clear that she had made it home from work; the two slices of pizza she had bought were found inside her refrigerator and her Publix uniform was neatly folded on her bed.

Detectives learned that Ali had taken a phone call at 12:48 am on Friday; although they refused to release the caller's name during the early stages of the investigation, the call helped narrow down the time of her disappearance. Like James, she had failed to show up for her marriage counseling session early that morning, leading investigators to believe that something had happened to her overnight.

Suspicion immediately fell on Ali's estranged husband. A neighbor saw a car in Ali's driveway around 7:30 am Friday, and he told police that he believed it belonged to James. Detectives interrogated James several times, but he staunchly denied having been at Ali's home that morning and swore he had nothing to do with her disappearance. He voluntarily underwent a voice-stress test; the analyzer determined he was telling the truth. It was enough for police to refrain from publicly naming him as a suspect, but he remained a person of interest.

By the following week, the investigation seemed in danger of stalling. Despite several public appeals, investigators received few tips and had been unable to develop any solid leads. A letter sent to the editor of the Tallahassee Democrat decried the fact that there had been little media coverage of the case, pointing out that another pregnant woman, Laci Peterson, had made national news when she disappeared in 2002. The letter-writer was justifiably upset that Ali's case wasn't even getting local attention, let alone national.

Those who were close to Ali were devastated by her disappearance. Nine of her family members traveled to Tallahassee to help in the search; they planned to stay until Ali was located. They spent long hours canvassing the surrounding neighborhoods with missing flyers, making sure that every resident was aware of the fact that Ali was missing.

On February 10th, police held a press conference to update the public on their investigation. There was little to report. Several of Ali's family members spoke at the news conference, pleading for help in finding the missing woman while clinging tightly to photos of her. Later that night around 150 of Ali's relatives, friends, and coworkers held a candlelight vigil in front of her home. They shared stories about her, cried, and prayed for her safe return.

Forensic investigators returned to Ali's home a few days later, searching desperately for anything they might have missed during the initial investigation. Once again, they came up empty. Whatever had happened to Ali, it appeared that it hadn't happened inside her home.

At the end of February, the Tallahassee Police Department announced that they were offering a $10,000 reward for information leading to either Ali or the person responsible for her disappearance. It was the first time the department had ever offered such a reward in a missing person case, but they told reporters that they had little information to go on and were hoping the reward would help bring in new information to jumpstart the investigation.

Although Ali was still officially classified as a missing person, the fact that she had been gone for almost a month led detectives to conclude that she had most likely been a victim of foul play. In an effort to generate new leads, investigators gave interviews to several national television shows, including Dateline and Nancy Grace. Several new tips came in as a result of the increased publicity, but none of them led to any breaks in the case.

Four weeks after Ali vanished, James made his first public statement about the case. He said he was still having a hard time processing what had happened, and assured reporters that he had nothing to do with her disappearance. He didn't understand why people believed he would have done anything to harm Ali; he was adamant that they had still been in love and had been actively working towards a reconciliation. Officials admitted that James had been very cooperative with them, but stated that no one had been ruled out as a suspect.

In March, the reward for information was increased to $30,000. Hoping to increase the amount offered, one local business owner came up with an innovative way to collect money for the reward fund. Adam Bardhi, the owner of the Village Pizza & Pasta restaurant in Tallahassee, offered a discount on pizzas in exchange for donations to Tallahassee Crime Stoppers. Ali had been a frequent customer at his restaurant, and Adam wanted to do everything he could to make sure she wasn't forgotten.

Two months after Ali went missing, members of the Pensacola branch of the Klaas Kids Foundation, Escambia Search & Rescue of Pensacola, and Southeastern Canine Search & Rescue organized a large-scale search for her. Along with more than 150 volunteers, they spent two days combing through local neighborhoods, roadside ditches, and parts of the Apalachicola National Forest for clues that might lead to Ali's location. Any potential evidence they discovered was turned over to detectives from the Tallahassee Police Department to be analyzed, but nothing that was found helped advance the investigation.

With no new information coming in, the investigation soon stalled. It was excruciating for Ali's family and friends, especially as it grew closer to July 18th, the due date of the baby that Ali had wanted so badly. She should have been at home decorating the nursery and deciding on a name for her child, not missing without a trace. Instead of welcoming a new baby, Ali's relatives and friends spent July 18th dedicating a tree in her honor at Florida's Lake Ella.

Ali's case soon faded from the newspapers, with only an occasional mention on each anniversary of her disappearance. Investigators were tight-lipped about any progress that might have been made, saying only that they hadn't ruled out any suspects in the case. Many people still thought that James was behind his estranged wife's disappearance, but he continued to maintain his innocence. Although police hadn't officially ruled him out, they stated that he had always been cooperative in their investigation and there was nothing to indicate that he had done anything to Ali.

As time went by, more information about Ali's life in the days and months leading up to her disappearance became public knowledge and it started to seem unlikely that James had been involved in her disappearance. According to Ali's older sister, Tracy Smith, James hadn't been the only man in Ali's life. In October 2005, around the time James moved out of their home, Ali had attended FAMU's Homecoming festivities. There, she met 25-year-old Dwight Aldridge and the two started seeing each other. The relationship turned sexual, and due to the timing, Ali wasn't sure if Dwight or James was the father of her unborn child.

In July 2009, Tracy shared some emails she received from her sister with the Tallahassee Democrat. In a November 2005 email, Ali said that Dwight had attended an ultrasound appointment with her; she seemed to believe that he was likely the father of her baby. Despite this, she seemed to indicate that she wanted to reconcile with her husband.

In another email, dated December 20, 2005, Ali seemed to insinuate that there was some tension between her and Dwight. She wrote that although the two were still in frequent contact and saw each other a few times a week, Dwight, who had initially appeared to be excited about becoming a father, felt that the pregnancy had changed Ali too much.

When reporters asked Dwight about Ali, he denied that they had ever had a romantic relationship, claiming they were friends and nothing more. He refused to discuss her disappearance, saying only that it had been a long time ago and he had no idea when he had last spoken to Ali.

Years went by, and Ali's case remained unsolved. It wasn't until October 2021 that detectives announced that they had a prime suspect in the case: Dwight Aldridge. For the first time, they told the public that the 12:48 am call Ali had received on the night she vanished had been from Dwight. When questioned, he had admitted to making the call but claimed that he had been out of town at the time and denied having anything to do with Ali's disappearance. Investigators said they could prove that Dwight had lied to them; his cell phone records showed that he had been in Ali's neighborhood when he made the 12:48 am call.

According to investigators, Dwight still resided in the Tallahassee area in 2021 but had long since stopped cooperating with their investigation. Although they believe that Dwight most likely killed Ali, they are still struggling to come up with the evidence needed to make a solid case against him. As of December 2024, Ali's body still hasn't been found and she remains listed as a missing person.

Ali Gilmore was 30 years old when she disappeared in 2006. She was four months pregnant with her first child, and she was looking forward to becoming a mother. She was a friendly and compassionate woman who was always smiling, and she is deeply missed by her family and large circle of friends. Due to the circumstances surrounding her disappearance, detectives believe that she met with foul play; she was likely killed on the same day she disappeared. If you have any information that could lead to the recovery of Ali or aid in convicting her killer, please contact the Tallahassee Police Department at 850-891-4200 or Tallahassee Crime Stoppers at 850-574-8477.

MARTHA LEANNE GREEN

Martha Leanne Green finished her shift at the Holiday Inn in Dickson, Tennessee around 9:00 pm on Wednesday, April 15, 1987. The 17-year-old, who preferred to be called by her middle name, had arranged to be picked up from work by her twin brother, Lawson Green. Lawson borrowed his cousin's 1979 Monte Carlo and was waiting outside the hotel when Leanne got done. The drive from the Holiday Inn to the twins' home in White Bluff, Tennessee was only about 10 miles, but it soon became clear that they weren't going to get there quickly; they were only a mile into the drive when the Monte Carlo ran out of gas.

Lawson managed to guide the car onto the shoulder of Highway 46 and turn on the vehicle's hazard lights. As he and Leanne discussed what they should do, a car pulled in behind them to see if they needed any assistance. The car's occupants, a family of four who were on their way home from a Wednesday night church service, offered to drive the twins to the nearest gas station. Lawson accepted their offer, but Leanne was hesitant. Lawson tried to assure her that everything would be fine but she refused to get into the family's car. She told Lawson that she would wait with their vehicle while he went to get gas.

Realizing that nothing was going to change his sister's mind, Lawson left her sitting in the passenger seat of the Monte Carlo while he caught a ride to the gas station. When Lawson was dropped back off at the car less than 10 minutes later, however, there was no sign of Leanne. There were no clues indicating what had happened to the teenager and she was never seen again.

When Lawson checked inside the Monte Carlo, he found Leanne's purse along with the keys to the vehicle. There was no sign of a struggle inside or around the car; Leanne had simply disappeared. Lawson wasn't sure what he should do, so he returned home to his parents and they called the police.

Deputies from the Dickson County Sheriff's Department immediately determined that Leanne was missing under suspicious circumstances; they believed she had been abducted from the side of the road. The Monte Carlo had run out of gas on Highway 46 in the city of Pomona, and Lawson had parked it near where the railroad tracks crossed the highway. Police combed through the surrounding area but found no clues to Leanne's whereabouts.

Investigators made a public appeal for information, hoping that someone who had been driving on Highway 46 around the time Leanne went missing might have seen something, They asked for anyone who had seen a second vehicle pulled over near the Monte Carlo to contact detectives immediately, but only a few tips were received.

By Friday, Leanne's family was growing increasingly desperate to learn what had happened to the teenager. Her father, George Green, was asked by reporters if he could think of anyone who would have wanted to hurt his daughter, but he couldn't think of anyone. Leanne was a friendly and popular young woman who went to church with her family every Sunday and enjoyed taking care of children. She was a junior at Dickson High School and she got along well with her teachers and classmates.

Family friend Gilbert Taylor attended the same

church as the Greens and told reporters that everyone liked Leanne. "If I had to tell you in a few words about Leanne, she was a beautiful, young, outstanding lady." Leanne's mother, Margie Green, said her daughter never got into any kind of trouble. "She has never spent the night anywhere or ever gone anywhere for any length of time without me knowing where she was – even in broad daylight."

Leanne's junior prom was supposed to be held that week and she had been excited about going. She had saved money from her job at the Holiday Inn and purchased a pink prom dress with matching pink shoes and accessories. Blain Snyder, her prom date, said Leanne was quiet and extremely kind. "She went to church a lot. I don't think she had any enemies. She was just a real nice person...she is so different from everyone else I've dated."

Residents of White Bluff started collecting money so they could offer a reward for information leading to Leanne's recovery. Jamie Heath, a dispatcher for the Dickson County Sheriff's Department, admitted that they hadn't received any solid leads. "Everything's a dead end. Everybody's seen something but nobody's seen anything. I wish I could tell you different, but everything's come up a dead end so far. There's nothing to report."

Around 60 volunteers assisted in the search for Leanne; they spent two days scouring Dickson County for any sign of the missing teenager. By Friday night, they were starting to lose hope that she was going to be found. Fritz Sander, the rescue wilderness chief of the Dickson County Rescue Squad, had helped coordinate the search. He was confident that Leanne was not in any of the areas that had been covered by the search teams, which included a 10-mile area surrounding where her car was found.

On Saturday, the search teams branched out, combing more than 20 miles of roads in Dickson County and neighboring Hickman County. Blain joined the search party, while George traveled to Hickman County and spent the day distributing flyers with his daughter's picture on them. Detectives followed up on a few potential sightings of the missing teenager but were unable to confirm any of them.

Margie sat at home and listened to a police scanner, praying that she would hear word that her daughter had been found. Sunday was Easter, and she hoped that Leanne would be home in time to celebrate the holiday. "Oh, Lord…wouldn't it be wonderful if they find her before Sunday. Then we could praise God."

The physical search for Leanne was called off Saturday night. Searchers had spent three days scouring the area but failed to find a single clue as to what had happened to Leanne. Dickens County Detective Jerry Hayes admitted that foul play was the most likely scenario. "We feel she's been abducted. She's not the type of girl who would run off."

Detectives received a tip that a wine-colored Ford had been seen in the area where Leanne disappeared; it wasn't much to go on, but it was one of the few potential leads investigators had and they asked for help from the public in identifying the car.

A week after Leanne vanished, police set up a roadblock on Highway 46 near where the Monte Carlo had run out of gas. Detectives stopped each car that drove on that portion of the highway between 8:45 pm and 10:00 pm, hoping to find someone who had been driving on it at the same time the previous week. They found several potential witnesses and arranged to bring them in for formal interviews.

Investigators continued to interview people and follow up on potential leads for the next several weeks, but they still weren't sure what had happened to Leanne. Her family was devastated by her disappearance and struggled to adjust to life without her. George admitted that the family had been forced to put their lives on hold. "We just live one day at a time. We've dropped everything to concentrate on this." As Mother's Day approached, Margie wanted no other gift than to have her daughter back home. Sadly, the day passed without any progress on Leanne's case.

Leanne's twin brother seemed to take her disappearance the hardest. Lawson opted not to return to school that year; a homebound teacher checked in on him weekly so he could complete his assignments without having to leave his house. Margie noted, "He doesn't say too much, but by his actions, I know he feels somewhat responsible. We just try to tell him it could have happened wherever she went. It could happen to anyone."

Detectives continued to believe that Leanne had been abducted, and the Tennessee Bureau of Investigation as well as the FBI were assisting the Dickson County Sheriff's Department in the investigation. Although everyone was hoping that Leanne would be found alive, investigators admitted that their hope grew a little dimmer each day.

Margie was certain that Leanne wouldn't have willingly gotten into a car with a stranger; she believed Leanne had either been forced into a vehicle by someone with a weapon or she had been enticed by someone she knew and trusted. Detectives had interviewed everyone within Leanne's social circle, however, and didn't believe any of them were responsible. Although stranger abductions were exceedingly rare, investigators feared that was what they were dealing with in this case.

By May 10, 1987, the reward for information had grown from $500 to $5,000, and more donations continued to come in. Leanne's family was grateful for the support of the community; they thanked everyone for donating both their time and money to the search effort. Margie said that everyone's support was helping the family cope with the situation.

On May 13, 1987, the Tennessee Bureau of Investigation set up a tip line specifically for Leanne's case; anyone who had any information was asked to call and speak with an investigator. TBI Agent John Carney admitted that they were setting up the tip line because they were running out of leads. "We're getting to a point where we're not getting much information." The reward in the case was up to $8,500, and detectives were hopeful that this might entice someone to call.

Agent Carney stated that detectives had run down more than 200 investigative leads but none of them brought them any closer to Leanne. They were still in the process of checking on a number of vehicles that had been seen in the vicinity of the Monte Carlo. "There were some people who stopped, and some individuals who were on the scene but have not come forward yet." While he believed it was likely most of these people had offered assistance and then drove off when Leanne declined, detectives still wanted to talk to them.

Through interviews with other drivers, Agent Carney noted, "Detectives have the abduction time narrowed down to 5 to 7 minutes. It's absolutely frustrating." Investigators were looking at similar cases from Oklahoma and Arkansas to see if there were any links; all involved young women who appeared to have been abducted from their car on a highway.

Two months after Leanne vanished, Margie said she was still holding on to the hope that she would be found alive. "We released a bunch of balloons today with her flyer in them...I just know there's someone somewhere who knows something."

In August 1987, officials announced that they had identified a potential suspect in Leanne's abduction. Robert Richards, a 22-year-old from Memphis, Tennessee, was suspected of abducting and murdering Teresa Butler in November 1986. Teresa, a 26-year-old nursing student from Memphis, went missing while driving home from a shift at a Memphis hospital. Her car was found abandoned on a rural road; the car was still running when it was found. Teresa was still missing and presumed dead.

Robert Richards became a suspect in Teresa's case after he was arrested for impersonating a police officer and attempting to abduct a young woman in Hardeman County. The positioning of Teresa's car when it was found suggested that she had likely been pulled over, though there was no record of any law enforcement officer in the area at the time she went missing. Detectives theorized that Richards had likely pulled her over by pretending to be a cop, then abducted and killed her. It was possible he had used the same ruse to get Leanne out of the Monte Carlo.

Agent Carney wasn't so sure Richards was the man he was looking for but agreed to send a detective to question him while he was being held in a Memphis jail. "I think law enforcement officials in Shelby and Hardeman Counties have over-exaggerated the possibility of Richards' involvement with Leanne." He noted that they had no concrete evidence linking him to the crime but he was willing to look into the possibility.

Richards allegedly told a friend that he had raped

and killed a 16-year-old girl with brown hair; although some investigators believed that this could have been Leanne, who was 17 years old when she vanished, others noted that Richards had made several contradicting statements and it was unclear if anything he said was the truth.

While in custody, Richards confessed to killing Teresa Butler, but he later recanted his confession and investigators were unable to find her body. Detectives were also having trouble linking him to Leanne. Dickson County Deputy Tom Wall admitted, "We haven't been able to put Richards in our county...the nearest we can put him in our area right now is in May in Hickman County."

By October 1987, Leanne had been missing for six months and her family had accepted the fact that they likely weren't going to find her alive. Margie wanted the killer to be found. "I hope it's handled in such a way that he will be punished because of this. Leanne was minding her own business and someone snatched her up and snuffed out her life at 17."

Deputy Wall admitted that the case was frustrating. "We don't have anything new...[and] we've put more time and manpower into this case than anything in the history of Dickson County." Detectives were still trying to link Richards to the case but hadn't had any luck finding any solid evidence.

Soon it was April again and Leanne's family marked the grim first anniversary of her disappearance. There had been little progress on the case, though Dickson County District Attorney General Kenneth Atkins said it remained a priority. "The TBI administered a polygraph test a few weeks ago in this case, but it didn't turn up anything good for us. They did some diving a week or so back, but nothing was found. We're just covering all the bases."

While he was in jail, Robert Richards told officials that he killed Leanne and could lead them to her body. He then proceeded to give a number of conflicting statements about where she was buried; detectives followed up on each one but were unable to locate Leanne. Assistant District Attorney Dan Cook believed Richards was most likely lying. "There's absolutely no evidence to indicate that this individual was responsible for her disappearance." He thought that Richards was falsely confessing because it allowed him to spend time outside of jail as he tried to lead investigators to Leanne's body. "There are people who will do or say anything to get out for a few days."

On October 27, 1990, Leanne's family held a memorial service for her. Margie noted, "It's not because we've discovered anything new about her whereabouts, but it will help us vent our grief."

Robert Richards was murdered in prison on July 21, 1991. If he was the person responsible for Leanne's abduction and murder, he took his knowledge of her burial spot to his grave. He had spent the four years leading up to his death admitting and then denying that he had anything to do with Leanne's disappearance; he seemed to enjoy the attention he got from detectives whenever he would offer a confession. Investigators remain divided on whether or not he was the person who abducted Leanne and they continue to search for her body.

Martha Leanne Green was just 17 years old when she went missing from Highway 46 outside of White Bluff, Tennessee in April 1987. She was a sweet and friendly girl who was looking forward to going to her junior prom that week, but the experience was stolen from her by an unknown person. Leanne has green eyes and brown hair, and at the time of her disappearance, she was 5 feet 6 inches tall and weighed 120 pounds. She was last seen wearing blue jeans, a white sweatshirt, and white high-top sneakers; she was also wearing brown-tinted contact lenses. Leanne's ears were pierced and she has a birthmark on her chest. If you have any information about Leanne, please contact the Dickson County Sheriff's Department at 615-789-4130 or the Tennessee Bureau of Investigation at 615-952-4989.

ANGELA HAMBY

Angela Hamby left her Wilkesboro, North Carolina home at 9:30 am on Friday, October 29, 1982, to run a few errands. The 20-year-old had taken the day off from work and had several errands to run. She planned to fill up her gas tank, take a deposit to a local bank for her mother, and then pay her car payment before returning home so she and her mother could go shopping in Elkin, North Carolina. She never picked her mother up, however, and she was never seen again.

When Angela failed to return home, her mother, Shirley, wasn't initially worried. She knew Angela planned to stop by her sister's house to see if she wanted to come along on their shopping trip; at first, she thought Angela and her sister, Cheryl, had simply started talking and lost track of time. Around noon, Shirley called Cheryl and was disturbed to find out that Angela had never arrived at her home, which was located near the bank. Concerned, Shirley called the bank next and learned that Angela hadn't been there yet.

Shirley drove to the bank in downtown Wilkesboro and looked around to see if she could spot Angela's silver Mazda. Hoping that Angela had met up with some friends, her mother decided to wait a few more hours to see if she showed up. Angela's father, Jerry, was on a hunting trip in South Carolina at the time and Shirley didn't want to worry him over nothing, but by 5:00 pm she was concerned enough that she called Jerry and then called the Wilkesboro Police Department to report Angela missing.

Around 1:00 am Saturday, a Wilkesboro police officer found Angela's car. It had been parked behind a dumpster in a small parking lot between the ABC store and the Tastee Freeze at the intersection of Main Street and Curtis Bridge Road. The car had a full tank of gas, indicating that Angela had made it to the gas station when she left her house. The driver's side door had been left unlocked, something that Angela never did. Her purse, wallet, and identification were found inside her car, but the money she had been carrying to take to the bank was missing.

A witness told detectives he had seen the car pull into the parking lot around 11:30 am Friday; he thought there had been a white male behind the wheel. Other witnesses claimed to have seen Angela driving her car in the area that morning, so it's unclear exactly who was driving the car when it was abandoned. One person thought they saw her shopping in a clothing store; they claimed she was looking around nervously, as if she were trying to avoid someone.

A cook who worked at the Tastee Freeze told investigators that she had seen Angela in the parking lot Friday morning; she had been speaking with a blond man whom the cook didn't recognize. She described the man as being "sort of rough looking" and wasn't sure if Angela knew him, but the two appeared to be talking and there were no signs of tension.

Police searched the downtown area but didn't find any sign of Angela. Her friends and family were adamant that she wouldn't have voluntarily disappeared; she had a strong relationship with her parents and enjoyed her job as a data processor for a bank. She was taking classes at Wilkes Community College and wanted to transfer to Appalachian State University to complete her degree.

Angela had been dating a young man from Valdese, North Carolina, a small town about an hour away from Wilkesboro. She was supposed to meet him the next day for a planned trip to Cherokee, North Carolina; she had been excited about the trip and her father didn't think she would have willingly missed it. "If she left on her own, it was a total reversal of character."

Jerry and Shirley spent the two days following their daughter's disappearance staring at the phone, praying it would ring with good news. As days went by without any word from Angela, they started taking long drives, searching up and down secluded country roads, looking for any place someone might have taken their daughter.

Soon, Wilkesboro was covered in Angela's missing person poster, and it was impossible to go anywhere downtown without seeing her picture. Although everyone in Wilkesboro was soon aware of the fact she was missing, none of them were able to offer any clues about where she might have gone. The North Carolina State Bureau of Investigation was brought in to assist the Wilkesboro detectives, but they weren't able to uncover any new leads.

Investigators wanted to identify the blond man seen driving Angela's car; they developed a composite sketch of the man based on the description provided by the Tastee Freeze cook. Angela's parents couldn't think of anyone their daughter knew who matched the description; they feared she had been abducted by a stranger.

Wilkesboro Police Sgt. Gary Parsons agreed that foul play was a possibility; since all of Angela's personal belongings had been left in her car, he thought she had likely been taken against her will. Her car was being processed by the state crime lab, but they hadn't found anything to indicate a struggle had taken place inside or around the vehicle. Despite the lack of evidence, those who knew Angela were convinced she never would have voluntarily left her car behind; she was still making payments on it and it was her prized possession.

As the search for Angela reached the two-week mark, her parents worried that they might never see her again. Shirley noted, "We've checked with friends of hers...we've checked everywhere. It is getting long, too long." There had been no confirmed sightings of Angela since the day she went missing, and everyone who knew her was growing increasingly concerned for her safety.

On November 17, 1982, Angela's parents announced that they were offering a $10,000 reward for information leading to their daughter's whereabouts. On the same day, Governor James Hunt's office announced that they were offering a $5,000 reward in the case. Detectives admitted that they had exhausted all available leads; they were hopeful that the reward money would entice someone with information to come forward and speak with them.

Investigators were still trying to find the blond man who had been seen with Angela the morning she disappeared, but no one seemed to know who he was. Angela's family found it hard to believe that she would have voluntarily let him drive her car; she didn't like anyone to borrow her car and would only rarely allow family members to use it.

In February 1983, detectives stated that there was a possibility Angela's disappearance was connected to a series of assaults against women that had taken place at hospitals in several North Carolina counties. Four women reported being assaulted by a suspect whose description was similar to that of the man seen driving Angela's car. One woman was abducted and raped, another was beaten by the man but managed to escape from his car, and two others were able to get away without injury. The suspect managed to evade authorities each time.

In March 1983, Jerry and Shirley Hamby filed to obtain control of their daughter's finances so they could pay her bills and take care of other financial matters until she was found. A lawyer working for them noted, "It's just a way of getting legal representatives to manage Angela's financial affairs until she shows up." The order was granted.

In April 1983, Shirley visited the parking lot where her daughter was last seen, still trying to comprehend how she could have vanished. "This sort of thing is supposed to happen at night. We're supposed to be afraid of the dark. But this happened in broad daylight, in a busy place with people all around. It doesn't make sense."

Shirley told reporters that her daughter had never been the adventurous type. She didn't suffer from wanderlust and had never yearned for independence. She was happiest at home with her parents or spending time with her boyfriend. "She called me every day. We worked different hours, but she always told me when she was leaving the house and when she got home. We were very close."

Everyone who knew Angela said she wasn't the type of person who would strike up a conversation with a stranger. Shirley noted, "Angie was real nervous. I know she never would have picked up a stranger. Somebody would have had to grab her." Although she was convinced her daughter had been abducted, Shirley was optimistic that she was still alive. "I'm sure Angela is not dead...I've dreamed of her, and they're always good dreams. I've never seen her dead in my dreams."

By April, the Wilkes County Sheriff's Office had

taken over the investigation. They hadn't made much progress, although they didn't believe that Angela had left voluntarily. Sheriff Kyle Gentry said that investigators had been frustrated by the lack of leads in the case. "It is really baffling. We sure wish something would turn up."

As the first anniversary of Angela's disappearance approached, detectives were still struggling to determine what had happened to her. Stephen Cabe, a detective with the State Bureau of Investigation, admitted, "It is a very puzzling case. There have been more man-hours spent on this case than any similar investigation that I know of, and still there is nothing."

Angela's family and friends continued to pray for her on a regular basis and constantly called the Wilkesboro Police Department for updates about the case. Officer Judy Gaylor said they never had anything new to report to Angela's loved ones. "I wish there was something we could tell them. It's still an open case, but we've reached a stumbling block and about all we can do is hope for a new lead."

Years went by without any solid leads and Angela remained missing. In April 1987, Wilkesboro Police Chief Gary Parsons told reporters that detectives had followed hundreds of leads but were no closer to determining what had happened to the missing woman. They had recently interviewed two men who were charged with murder in South Carolina, but Chief Parsons said they had been unable to connect the men to Angela's disappearance. When conducting a search of one man's home, investigators had found a clipping about Angela's disappearance, but he had been in jail at the time of her disappearance and there was no other evidence to link either man to Angela.

Angela's family had hoped that the two men,

Michael Ryan Torrence and Thomas John Torrence would be able to provide them with information about her fate and weren't sure how to take the news that they weren't involved. Jerry admitted, "I guess I was relieved. Apparently those guys are sort of rough customers. But I get to the point where I'd just like to know something, even if it was bad."

Unfortunately, Angela's case soon went cold. Detectives continued to look through the case file on a regular basis, hoping to find something that had been missed during the initial investigation, but they were unable to come up with any solid leads. The evidence collected from in and around Angela's Mazda – which included a plastic raincoat, cigarette butts, Angela's purse, and pieces of paper – were reevaluated several times, but they failed to lead police to the person responsible for Angela's disappearance. Her fate remains a mystery.

Angela Gray Hamby was just 20 years old when she vanished from Wilkesboro, North Carolina in October 1982. She was a shy young woman who preferred to stick close to home, and investigators believe she was abducted and likely murdered. Angela has blue eyes and blonde hair, and at the time of her disappearance, she was 5 feet 4 inches tall and weighed 105 pounds. She was last seen wearing blue jeans, a cream-colored V-neck sweater, an orchid-colored sweater, socks, and sandals. She also had on a sapphire and diamond ring and a gold bead necklace. If you have any information about Angela, please contact the Wilkes County Sheriff's Office at 336-838-9111 or the Wilkesboro Police Department at 336-667-7277.

ANGELA HAMMOND

It was around 11:15 pm on Thursday, April 4, 1991, when Angela Hammond called her fiancé, Rob Shafer, from a payphone in the parking lot of a Clinton, Missouri supermarket. Rob was babysitting his younger brother that night, and Angie had planned to meet up with him. The 20-year-old was four months pregnant, however, and she called to tell him she was tired and planned to go home and take a bath.

While she was on the phone with Rob, Angie noticed a man was circling the parking lot in an older model green pickup truck. When he stopped the truck near the payphone and got out, Angie quietly described him to Rob, noting he was wearing glasses and had a beard and mustache. He was carrying a flashlight with him and Angie thought he might be looking for something in the parking lot, but then he started walking in her direction.

The man walked up to the payphone next to the one Angie was using and lifted the receiver as if he were making a call but then hung it up immediately. Rob heard Angie ask the man if he needed to use the phone she was on; the man said he would try again later. He started to walk back toward his truck but then stopped and turned around. Angie whispered to Rob that the strange man was heading back in her direction; before Rob could reply, Angie screamed and the line went dead.

Terrified that his fiancé was in trouble, the 18-year-old jumped in his car and headed for the Food Barn parking lot, which was seven blocks from his home. As he raced down the street, he saw a green truck coming toward him. When it passed him, he could hear Angie screaming for help. He quickly turned around and tried to catch up with the truck, which he thought was a 1969 or 1970 Ford. He only made it about a mile when his car's transmission blew out, stranding him on the side of the road.

Rob made his way to a payphone and called the police, telling them everything that he knew about Angie's abduction. Although he didn't get a good look at the driver, he noticed that the green pickup truck had a decal of a nature or fishing scene covering its rear window; he also believed the truck had damage to its left front fender. Police scoured the area for any sign of the truck but were unable to find it.

Officers found Angie's car in the Food Barn parking lot near the payphone she had used to call Rob, but there was nothing to indicate what had happened to her. Witnesses recalled seeing a white male driving a truck near the payphone shortly before Angie was abducted, but they hadn't paid much attention to him so were unable to give a detailed description of him.

Angie wasn't the first young woman to disappear in Missouri that year and investigators worried that they might have a serial killer on their hands. In January, Trudy Darby was abducted from a convenience store in Macks Creek, Missouri, while in February, Cheryl Kenney was abducted from Nevada, Missouri shortly after she finished her job at a convenience store. Trudy was later found dead, but Cheryl was still missing. It seemed possible that someone was stalking business parking lots, looking for vulnerable women.

Since detectives immediately knew that Angie had been abducted, the FBI was brought in to assist in the investigation. FBI spokesman Jeff Lanza admitted there was a possibility the cases of the three women were related, but cautioned the public against jumping to conclusions as it was just one of a number of theories investigators were considering.

More than 250 volunteers helped local, state, and federal authorities search for Angie; by Sunday night, they had covered much of Henry County but had been unable to find any clues to her whereabouts. A search for the green pickup truck had also been fruitless.

Rob was extremely concerned for his fiancée's safety, especially since she was pregnant. He was trying to remain hopeful that Angie would be found alive but admitted it got harder to be optimistic as days went by without any progress in the investigation.

Friends described Angie as a friendly and outgoing young woman who was a lot of fun to be around. A graduate of Montrose High School, she was looking forward to becoming a mother and had already started buying things for the baby. Angie worked most evenings as a night processor at Union State Bank but had off the night she was abducted.

She and her best friend, Kyla Engeman, spent much of Thursday night driving around the small town of Clinton and hanging out with friends in the town square. Shortly after 11:00 pm, the friends had parted ways, with Kyla going home and Angie heading for a payphone so she could call Rob and tell him she was too tired to meet up with him later that night. Angie didn't have a telephone at home, so she was familiar with the locations of various payphones and used them frequently. She had never expressed any fears for her safety prior to this incident.

Detectives obtained phone records from the payphone and determined that Angie called Rob at 11:13

pm and spoke with him until around 11:45 pm. They hoped to find witnesses who might have seen a green pickup truck in the area while Angie was on the phone.

Clinton Police Detective Damon Parsons admitted that he feared for Angie's welfare, noting that the chances of finding her alive were slim. He also noted that no one had been eliminated as a possible suspect in the case; investigators were still in the process of interviewing everyone associated with Angie to see if they could think of anyone who might have wanted to harm her.

A few days after Angie went missing, her fiancé and one of her ex-boyfriends both agreed to take polygraph examinations about her disappearance. Bill Barker, a 17-year-old who had dated Angie before she started seeing Rob in late 1990, said he was questioned for about three hours. "I guess they were just trying to clear us as suspects...they were asking why we would do something like this to her."

Rob was questioned by FBI agents for more than five hours. "They don't think my story's any good...I told them everything I know." Detectives wouldn't discuss the polygraph results but said that Rob and Bill had been questioned primarily as witnesses who had known Angie well. Eventually, both young men were cleared of suspicion.

On April 15, 1991, detectives enlisted the help of the Missouri Rural Crime Squad. Detective Parsons said they had exhausted all available leads and still had no idea exactly what had happened to Angie; they were hoping the extra resources would help them find Angie or the green pickup truck driven by her abductor.

Angie's mother, Marsha Cook, said she was happy to learn that the crime squad would be helping detectives. "They're not sitting still...they're still working on it, so we're very pleased. We've more or less left the investigation up to the police, and they've been wonderful."

Union State Bank where Angie worked announced that they were offering a $5,000 reward for information leading to Angie or the arrest and conviction of the person responsible for her disappearance. Another local bank also set up a reward fund; a week after Angie's disappearance, they had collected $600.

As the search for Angie entered its third week, officials asked for help from the public. Residents in rural areas of west-central Missouri were asked to check their properties, including any outbuildings, for anything suspicious that might help detectives locate the missing woman. They also noted that the owner of the pickup truck might have abandoned it after all the publicity surrounding Angie's abduction; it was possible it was dumped on someone's property without their knowledge.

As news of Angie's disappearance spread, new witnesses reached out to detectives. Two women said they saw Angie using the payphone the night she vanished; they initially thought she was one of their friends so they pulled into the Food Barn parking lot to talk to her. As they got closer, they realized it wasn't their friend and started to drive away. As they did, they saw a man sitting in a green pickup truck; he leaned back in his seat as if he didn't want them to see his face. Detectives believed Angie was abducted right after the women drove away.

After interviewing several people who thought they saw the pickup truck driven by Angie's abductor, detectives announced that they were looking for a 1968 to 1970 Ford truck with a color decal of a fishing scene covering the rear window. The truck was light green on its bottom half and dark green on its top half, with a strip of chrome separating the two colors. The truck also had a white roof, and its license plate may have contained the letters "XY." The driver was a white male, 20 to 35 years old, with dark, collar-length hair and a mustache. He had a medium build and was wearing a dark-colored T-shirt and a baseball cap; the witnesses all said he was dirty in appearance.

A month after Angie was last seen, the reward for information was up to $11,000 as detectives struggled to develop any solid leads in the case. They had followed up on more than 500 tips but none of them brought them any closer to finding Angie. Clinton Police Chief Bob Pattison said detectives weren't going to give up until Angie was located. "We're staying right on it. We're still looking for the vehicle, for the suspect, and for Angela. There's been nothing really solid, though."

Angie's mother was trying to stay positive. "I'm trying to prepare myself for the worst and yet trying to hope for the best. I'm taking it one day at a time…until they find something, I'm trying to stay optimistic." Hoping to bring in some new leads, Angie's grandparents, Lloyd and Elizabeth Young, offered an additional $5,000 reward for information about her whereabouts.

Even with the increased reward, Angie's case soon went cold. Months went by, and investigators admitted they didn't know anything more than they had on the night Angie disappeared. In October 1991, Marsha admitted that it didn't look as if her daughter was going to be found alive, but she was still hoping for a miracle. "I know the statistics aren't good at this point for finding her, but until something happens, you can't give up."

Detective Parsons stated that investigators still had no idea what had happened to Angie. "There's someone out there who has information…they just may not realize it. Until they come forward, or until she's found, there really is not much more we can do."

In December 1991, investigators received a tip that Angie had been seen in Selkirk, Manitoba, Canada. A man named Russell Smith was certain that he had seen the missing woman in September; he claimed she walked out of a drugstore and got into a green truck with a white top and a mural in the rear window. "I know that I saw the girl. I know that for a fact...I never forget a face."

Detectives said they did not doubt that Russell believed he had seen Angie but they had been unable to confirm the sighting. Since Angie should have had her baby by the time Russell saw her, Canadian authorities distributed Angie's missing flyer to local hospitals, birthing centers, and infant clothing stores, but no one recalled seeing her.

On January 29, 1992, Angie's case was featured on an episode of the television show "Unsolved Mysteries." Detectives – and Angie's loved ones – were hopeful that the national exposure would bring in some new leads and reinvigorate the investigation, which had been stalled for months.

In the days following the "Unsolved Mysteries" episode, investigators received 387 calls from people who believed they had information about Angie or her abductor. By the end of the week, the number would rise to more than 600. It would take time for detectives to wade through all the tips but they followed up on each one. None of them led to Angie.

In April 1993, police used cadaver dogs to search a farm in Lafayette County, Missouri after a psychic claimed that Angie was buried there. Detectives said they didn't usually launch searches based on psychic hunches, but they had questioned a man who used to live at the property in the past after receiving a tip he had a truck similar to the one used in Angie's abduction.

An informant claimed the man had a green pickup truck at one time and it was supposedly buried on the Lafayette County property. Detectives searched the area and found some car parts but nothing that came from a truck. A few weeks after they completed their initial search, a reporter for a Clinton newspaper took a psychic to the property and she claimed Angie had been held there.

Chief Pattison admitted he was skeptical. "I don't have any faith in psychics. The particular person that's being looked at as a possible suspect, we've 95 percent cleared him…he has a pretty good alibi. He took a lie detector test and we feel like he passed it." Rumors that Angie's body was somewhere on the property continued to spread throughout Clinton, however, so investigators decided to bring in cadaver dogs to settle the issue.

Around two dozen investigators from the Lafayette County Sheriff's Office and five cadaver dogs spent several hours combing through the 60-acre property. The dogs didn't react to anything and the search turned up no clues to Angie's whereabouts.

Angie's case gradually faded from the headlines as the investigation stalled. Years went by without any significant developments; although detectives continued to receive sporadic tips about the case, they still didn't know exactly what had happened to the missing woman. Despite the passage of time, Clinton Police Sgt. Paul Abbott insisted the case wasn't cold. "We've been working on this case diligently for the last 18 years."

Marsha told reporters she knew her daughter was most likely dead but she wanted her body to be found so she could give her a proper burial and obtain some degree of closure. As hard as it would be for her to know Angie had been killed, the uncertainty was worse. Marsha praised the detectives working on the case, stating that they were wonderful about keeping her updated on the status of the investigation.

As the 30th anniversary of Angie's disappearance approached in 2021, the Clinton Police Department released new information that seemed to suggest Angie's abduction was a case of mistaken identity. The lead centered around a confidential informant who aided police in a sting operation targeting a large narcotics ring. This man, who had been assigned a confidential number to protect his identity during the court case, received a letter postmarked April 4, 1991, at the home where he was staying in Clinton, Missouri. The sender addressed the man by his confidential number and wrote, "We know where your foxy daughter is at...she will see us soon." This man's daughter was named Angela.

Detectives believed that Angie might have been abducted after being mistaken for the confidential informant's daughter. They said they had recently received additional information that made them believe this was a credible theory; an anonymous person had called and given them the names of two people who were possibly involved. They pleaded with this person to contact them again, promising to protect his identity. If this man did reach back out to detectives, they didn't inform the public.

As of December 2024, Angie remains listed as a missing person. There are many theories about what might have happened to her that April night more than three decades ago, but with little evidence to prove any theory, detectives have been unable to move forward. Some people believe she was abducted by someone who just happened to be driving by and saw her alone in a parking lot and took advantage of her vulnerable state. Others think it was a case of mistaken identity, while still others whisper that her boyfriend was somehow involved – despite the fact that police have said he was cleared as a suspect. Sadly, until someone confesses or Angie's body is found, we may never know the truth.

Angela Marie Hammond was just 20 years old when she was abducted from a Clinton, Missouri parking lot in April 1991. Angie was four months pregnant at the time and engaged to be married; she had a bright future and a lot to look forward to, but this was stolen from her by a person who has never been identified. Angie has brown eyes and brown hair, and at the time of her disappearance, she was 5 feet tall and weighed 140 pounds. She was last seen wearing black pants, a white button-down shirt with black polka dots, and white sneakers. If you have any information about Angie, please contact the Clinton Police Department at 660-885-5561.

ALLAN KAPLAN

Allan Kaplan left the Banana Boat Lounge in Boca Raton, Florida around 2:00 am on Friday, December 9, 1977. The 39-year-old, a successful restauranteur who was the president of Allan Kaplan Restaurants Inc., left the lounge with 19-year-old model Sharon Wead, but the two got into separate cars and drove off in different directions when they pulled out of the parking lot. Allan headed back to his apartment in nearby Boynton Beach, Florida, but what happened after he arrived there is unclear; he failed to show up for work in the morning and he was never seen again.

Hugh Merrill, the assistant manager of Mark XV, one of Allan's restaurants, reported him missing on Monday after discovering that no one had spoken to him since he left the Banana Boat Lounge. The Palm Beach County Sheriff's Office took the missing person report but initially believed that Allan had likely left on his own. Four days after Allan was last seen, one of his restaurants was broken into and $4,000 was missing from the safe. Detectives thought it was likely that Allan had taken the money and run off with it. After investigating, however, they determined that the theft had likely been committed by someone else.

Palm Beach County Detective Charles Fortunato found Allan's car in the parking lot of his apartment building, but there was no sign of Allan. When he searched Allan's apartment, he noticed a few things that concerned him. "All of his friends say he was a very tidy guy, but when we went into the apartment, we found clothes and hangers on the floor and the bed hadn't been made." The detective's concern grew when he noticed several things that Allan had left behind. "He left his briefcase that contained important papers, his passport, and a ticket to the Bahamas." He had recently bought a new car, and it was found parked in its usual spot in the apartment complex's parking lot.

Investigators spoke with Allan's neighbors and found one woman who recalled hearing his apartment door slam shut around 7:00 am on Friday morning, about five hours after Allan had left the Banana Boat Lounge. Detective Fortunato said that the neighbor hadn't seen if Allan was the person who slammed the door. "The question is, what happened to Kaplan if that was him leaving the apartment? Did he leave willingly with someone else, did he just walk away, or was he kidnapped?"

After interviewing Sharon Wead and the bartender who had been working at the Banana Boat Lounge the night Allan went missing, detectives were certain that Allan had made it back to his apartment safely. Both Sharon and the bartender were able to identify the clothing that Allan had been wearing; the items were found in his apartment, indicating he had gotten changed after arriving home. What happened after that remained a mystery.

Sharon, who had been one of the last people to speak with Allan, told investigators that he had already been at the Banana Boat Lounge when she and a friend arrived there late on the evening of December 8, 1977. There had only been one open seat at the bar, and Allan had gotten up so that Sharon and her female friend could sit together. The three had chatted for a while, and Allan had escorted Sharon to her car when the bar closed. "He'd been at the bar before me, but he walked out perfectly normal. He was a perfect gentleman."

Allan's neighbors didn't know him very well; they told detectives that he was a quiet man who worked long hours and seemed to keep to himself. When he wanted to relax, he would spend a few days in the Bahamas.

Three weeks after Allan was last seen, detectives hadn't made any progress on the case. Detective Fortunato told reporters that he believed Allan had been a victim of foul play. "We don't have any evidence that he has met with foul play or that he would take his own life. But at this point, we have to think that something has happened to him. He would have told someone he was leaving or contacted someone by now...things just don't add up."

Allan was divorced and his ex-wife lived in California with the couple's two daughters. She told detectives that he failed to send his children any presents for Christmas, something he had always done in the past. He had also failed to contact a woman he was dating who lived in Ohio. She said that Allan frequently traveled to the Bahamas, but he would always let her know before he left. They had plans to get together during the holidays, but she hadn't heard from him since he went missing.

Investigators made a public appeal for information about Allan, and they received dozens of tips. Unfortunately, they were unable to develop any substantial leads and Detective Fortunato admitted that they had no idea what had happened to him. "It's a weird case. We know a lot about his family and his work, but we know next to nothing about his private life. He could have been involved in the Mafia or leaving for the priesthood."

A month after Allan vanished, Detective Fortunato

was struggling to make sense of his disappearance. "There are all kinds of theories, but that's our problem. We can't find any reason for him to take off or for anyone to do anything to him."

Allan had moved to Florida in June 1977; prior to that, he had been a restaurant consultant in Ohio. He purchased two restaurants in Boca Raton from an Akron, Ohio company that had filed for bankruptcy. Both restaurants were doing well at the time of Allan's disappearance; it didn't appear he had a financial motive to disappear. Although the original owner of the restaurants had filed for bankruptcy, within a couple of months Allan had turned both businesses around and each one was quite profitable when he vanished. He had ample money in the bank, but neither his bank accounts nor his credit cards had been touched since he went missing.

Seven months after Allan was last seen, detectives still weren't sure what had happened to him. Palm Beach County Detective Fred Mascaro told reporters, "We have no reason to think it wasn't foul play...the case is at a standstill."

After learning that Allan frequently flew to the Bahamas, detectives considered the possibility that he was involved in drug trafficking. They were unable to find any evidence of this, and those who knew Allan best were certain that he hadn't dabbled in any illegal activity. Detective Mascaro stated, "Everything's been gone through extensively. His whole background has been checked."

Detective Mascaro admitted that the case was starting to go cold. "The case is just dead. We don't know what happened. He could be in a morgue as a John Doe somewhere around the country, but we may never know."

Years went by and Allan's fate remained a mystery.

In 1986, Detective Mascaro told reporters that the case was one of the most baffling of his career. "That case is going to haunt me for 100,000 years. His background never showed any major criminal activity...nobody inherited a lot of money from life insurance policies. Thus, our leads for suspects were minimal." The lack of tips had been frustrating. "I wish I knew what happened to that man. He disappeared off the face of the earth."

Allan's ex-wife, Barbara, told reporters that she was certain he had been murdered as there was no way he would have willingly abandoned his daughters. "It's still a really sad thing. I don't think my kids have ever come to terms with it. It's difficult."

Allan Terry Kaplan was 39 years old when he went missing from Boynton Beach, Florida in December 1977. Allan had only been living in Florida for six months when he vanished; he had moved to the area from Ohio after buying two restaurants in Boca Raton, Florida. The circumstances surrounding his disappearance are murky and detectives admit they have no idea what happened to him, but they believe he was likely a victim of foul play. Allan has brown eyes and black hair, and at the time of his disappearance, he was 5 feet 10 inches tall and weighed 190 pounds. It's unclear what he was wearing when he went missing, but there was a suit missing from his apartment. He normally wore eyeglasses and one ring on each hand. If you have any information about Allan, please contact the Palm Beach County Sheriff's Office at 800-458-8477.

TRACY KROH

When Tracy Kroh left her Enterline Township, Pennsylvania home on the afternoon of Saturday, August 5, 1989, she didn't expect to be gone long. She planned to drive to her sister's home in nearby Halifax, Pennsylvania to return a barbeque grill she had borrowed and drop off some coupons she had clipped. Her sister, Tammy Hoffman, wasn't home when Tracy arrived, so she left the items on her front porch and returned to her car. She never made it back to her house.

Tracy's parents, Ivan and Ellen Kroh, weren't initially concerned when Tracy failed to come home that night. Tracy was very close with her sister and would often spend the night at her house, so Ellen assumed she had decided to stay over at Tammy's and would be back in the morning. When there was no sign of Tracy the following day, Ellen called Tammy and learned that Tracy hadn't spent the night with her. Ralph immediately got into his car and started driving around, looking for any sign of his daughter.

Ivan soon found Tracy's car, a 1971 Mercury Comet, parked and locked in front of Leppert's Five and Dime store in Millersburg Square, just a few minutes away from her sister's house. It was a popular gathering spot for teenagers, so Tracy's parents assumed that she had decided to meet up with some friends there on Saturday night. What happened after that was a mystery.

Tracy normally never went anywhere without letting her parents know where she was going to be; she was close with her parents and siblings and had no history of running away from home. Ellen told reporters that Tracy hadn't taken any of her belongings or cash with her when she left. "She had money upstairs, quite a bit of money. Her savings book is still here. She had her $8 allowance lying on the cupboard."

Tracy attended Halifax Area High School, where she was known as an excellent student and a talented artist. Dr. Wayne Boyer, the school district superintendent, noted, "She is an extremely responsible student, very hardworking and quiet. She has an excellent sense of humor. I could throw a joke out and she'd enjoy it."

Ellen stated that Tracy tended to stick close to home. "She didn't run around. She pretty much stayed home this past summer because she couldn't get a summer job." If she wasn't at home, she could usually be found at her sister's house.

Tracy was an artist for the school newspaper and the editor of the school yearbook; she had spent many hours over the summer working on the yearbook so everything would be in order when classes started in the fall. Classmates were certain that Tracy hadn't voluntarily disappeared, pointing out that she was very responsible and had big plans for the future. She was in the top 10 percent of her class and hoped to go to college to major in business.

Investigators and volunteers distributed missing person flyers throughout the area where Tracy's car was found, hoping to find someone who had seen the teenager after she left her sister's house. Ivan, who worked in the maintenance department of the Pennsylvania Turnpike Commission, handed out copies of Tracy's missing flyer to his co-workers, and they posted them along the entire length of the PA Turnpike.

Ellen admitted that she and Ivan immediately feared the worst. "The first thing that came to our minds was that someone took her. That was it. That was what we thought right away. But as far as thinking where she might be, all kinds of thoughts run through my mind." She worried that Tracy was being held somewhere against her will, perhaps being tortured or starved. The thoughts kept her awake at night.

Ivan took a week off from work so he could assist in the search for his daughter. Ellen stated, "I stayed by the phone, but my husband and the rest of the family and friends were out beating the roads...asking questions and showing her picture. But, no luck. Nobody had seen her."

As weeks went by without any sign of Tracy, her parents could only hope that she was still alive. While they prayed for her safe return, neighbors collected money to start a reward fund; by the end of September, they were able to offer a $5,000 reward for any information leading to Tracy's whereabouts. Pennsylvania Crime Stoppers offered an additional $1,000 for information, bringing the total to $6,000. Despite the monetary reward, investigators received few tips about the case.

Millersburg Police Chief Kenneth Rose admitted that investigators had no idea what had happened to Tracy. He told reporters that there had been no reported sightings of her since she was reported missing; although there was no evidence of foul play, he noted that it couldn't be ruled out.

Ellen was sure that someone had to know where her daughter was. "Someone's holding something back one way or the other. How can someone in Millersburg disappear without someone seeing something? I have the feeling somebody knows something and they're just afraid to say it."

Three weeks after Tracy vanished, there had been little progress made in her case. The Pennsylvania State Police had formed a task force to look into Tracy's disappearance, but they hadn't developed any solid leads. Ellen was frustrated. "Apparently, there is nothing to update, unfortunately. There might be things they are looking into, but they can't say, even to me...hope is the only thing I have left."

In January 1990, employees of MI Plastics in Millersburg donated money to have several large signs with Tracy's information erected in Millersburg and Halifax. They hoped that the signs would bring in some new tips for investigators to follow.

On March 18, 1990, scuba divers from New Cumberland River Rescue were sent to search a pond in Halifax after state police detectives received a tip that Tracy's body might be there. A total of a dozen divers spent two days searching the pond, which was about 70 yards wide and 14 feet deep. Pennsylvania State Police Cpl. Max Seiler told reporters that the pond was thoroughly searched for any evidence related to Tracy's case, but they came up empty. "Everything was negative."

Tracy's 18th birthday was April 16, 1990; it was a bittersweet day for her family. Ellen admitted, "She was on my mind the whole day...I would have normally been baking her a cake...it really hit me hard that day." In May, Tracy's classmates went to their senior prom, an event Tracy had been looking forward to attending.

Tracy should have been graduating from Halifax Area High School in June 1990, but the ceremony went on without her. Cpl. Richard Dressler admitted to reporters that the investigation was at a dead end. "There's been nothing, absolutely nothing, in the last month or so." A special task force from the state police barracks in

Harrisburg was continuing to assist in the case, but had been unable to determine what had happened to Tracy.

Ellen stated that she still believed someone in the area was withholding information about her daughter's disappearance. "I know darn well someone in Millersburg knows something. Someone can't just disappear in a small town."

By August 1990, Tracy had been missing for an entire year and police still didn't know what had happened to her. Although investigators said they couldn't rule out the possibility that Tracy ran away, it seemed unlikely and they believed she could have been a victim of foul play. Ellen was sure someone would have witnessed a struggle if Tracy had been abducted by a stranger, leading her to believe Tracy may have gotten into a car with someone she knew. "She wouldn't go with a stranger...if someone lured her away, it was somebody she thought was a friend."

Pennsylvania State Police Sgt. Lynn Hess told reporters that investigators had interviewed more than 100 people in the first few months following Tracy's disappearance, but none of them had been able to provide any clues to the teenager's whereabouts. "I'm still hopeful that we're going to be able to solve it. You don't know what is going to trigger the investigation and finally start tying the pieces of the puzzle together."

Three years after Tracy went missing, her picture was featured in a mass mailing that was sent by the National Center for Missing and Exploited Children to more than 50 million homes across the country. Tracy's family was pleased to learn that Tracy was going to be featured in the mailing; there hadn't been any leads in over a year and they were hopeful the mailing would bring in some new tips.

In September 1992, investigators received a tip from a jailhouse informant that convicted felon Larry Rampe was responsible for Tracy's disappearance. The informant, who had been housed in the Richmond City, Virginia jail with Rampe, told detectives that Rampe claimed he had abducted Tracy and buried her near Roanoke, Virginia. According to the informant, Rampe had kept Tracy's class ring as a souvenir.

Detectives followed up on the tip but soon ran into a few problems. Rampe had worked in Breezewood, Pennsylvania, a small town located two hours away from Millersburg, in 1989, but he hadn't been working there at the time Tracy went missing and there was no evidence he had been in the area. They searched his apartment in Virginia but found nothing connecting him to Tracy's case; eventually, they determined that the informant was unreliable.

On November 30, 1993, a farmer in Washington Township, Pennsylvania found Tracy's driver's license and National Honor Society wallet card on his property. Investigators determined that high water from Wiconisco Creek had washed the items onto the farmland. They scoured the area and found several photographs and other items related to the case, though they wouldn't comment on what these items were.

The items were sent to the state police crime laboratory for analysis. Sgt. Hess noted, "We want to determine the conditions the items have been exposed to over the years. This will give us more insight as to where they may have been. It helps to limit the scope of our search."

In April 1994, investigators conducted a search along Wiconisco Creek near where her driver's license and other items were found. State police were assisted by New

York's Adirondack Search and Rescue Team as well as a group of K-9 units. They didn't find anything useful to the investigation.

In May 1994, detectives received a tip that Tracy, along with two other missing women, was in Texas. The tipster claimed that Tracy, Beth Miller, who had gone missing from Colorado in 1982, and Tiffany Sessions, who went missing from Florida in 1989, were being held against their will and forced to work as prostitutes for a man named Thomas Stewart. Investigators followed up on the tip but were unable to confirm the information.

By August 1998, Tracy's trail had long gone cold. Pennsylvania State Police Cpl. Robert Mull did what he could to keep her case alive. "I have her on my wall looking at me. I get reminded of it every day, every time I come to work." He admitted that investigators hadn't had any substantial tips since her driver's license was found in 1993. "I think the rest of her wallet or her purse may be in that area. Maybe there are other possessions there, but it's such a vast area. We can't just go dig up someone's farm."

In December 2001, Dauphin County District Attorney Edward Marsico told reporters that he was optimistic that Tracy's case would soon be solved. "Information developed over the last few months has led to a renewed effort. Although we have not found a body or anything like that, we have reason to be hopeful." He noted that cadaver dogs had recently been used to search through an area of northern Dauphin County, but wouldn't discuss any potential finds.

D.A. Marsico admitted that they had ruled out the possibility that Tracy had voluntarily disappeared or been abducted by a stranger. "There was no way for a stranger to snatch her against her will in the center of Millersburg.

We believe her disappearance is tied closely to someone she knew. There is no prime suspect, but we have eliminated certain things."

Years went by, and there was no movement on the case. In December 2008, the Pennsylvania State Police erected a billboard along Route 225 in Halifax to remind the public that Tracy was still missing. The billboard included an age-progression photograph of Tracy to show what she might look like at age 35.

A new age-progression photo of how Tracy might look at age 42 was released in 2014 as the 25th anniversary of her disappearance approached. Although investigators said they had no new details to release to the public, Dauphin County Assistant District Attorney Fran Chardo told reporters, "After 25 years, we can say this was a criminal act that resulted in death...the circumstances of her death are such that she had every intention of returning and something prevented her from doing that. She was very close to her family."

In August 2019, 54-year-old Matthew Webster and Holly Mallett, both of Halifax, were arrested and charged with perjury for lying to a grand jury that had been convened to investigate Tracy's disappearance. Holly had initially told police Matthew discussed the rape and murder of Tracy with her in 2018. He denied the conversation ever took place, and was caught on wiretap coercing Holly to change her testimony, which she did. Both Holly and Matthew testified that they had no contact with each other prior to appearing in front of the grand jury, so the wiretaps were introduced as evidence and both were charged with perjury. No charges were filed in Tracy's disappearance.

According to investigators, Holly claimed that Matthew told her that he and some buddies had seen

Tracy in Millersburg Square the night she went missing. She said Matthew stated, "It was supposed to be just a rape and done, but then it turned out to be a lot more than that." Investigators searched a property in Halifax that had been owned by Matthew at the time of Tracy's disappearance, but they didn't find anything related to the case.

In May 2022, Pennsylvania State Trooper Jeremiah Mistick stated that 89-year-old Mark Eugene Warfel was under investigation for both Tracy's disappearance and the murder of his wife, Doris, as well as multiple sexual assaults. Warfel, who had been in prison since 2019 awaiting trial on burglary charges, was found not competent to stand trial and a judge ordered that he be released from custody.

Warfel had been friends with Tracy's parents for years and denied having anything to do with her disappearance. Tracy's sister, Kim, visited him in 2022 while he was in the hospital and secretly recorded the conversation. In it, he admits, "They put me in prison because I was connected with Tracy Kroh." He claimed that he didn't kill her, but that he knew who the murderer was. He said the killer dumped her body in a mine shaft.

In March 2023, Pennsylvania State Police spent 10 days conducting a controlled demolition of a home once owned by Warfel. They were hoping that they would find Tracy's body on the property. A spokesperson noted, "Two canine teams certified in human remains detection assisted in identifying primary excavation areas. Members meticulously excavated and searched the property, however, human remains were not discovered."

Warfel told reporters that he hadn't been concerned about the search, as he knew that detectives weren't going to find anything incriminating on his property. No charges have been filed against him as of December 2024, and Tracy is still listed as a missing person.

Tracy Marie Kroh was just 17 years old when she went missing from Millersburg, Pennsylvania in August 1989. She was an excellent student who was excited about starting her senior year of high school and was looking forward to going to college. Detectives believe that Tracy was abducted and murdered, but her body has never been found and no one has been charged in connection with her disappearance. Tracy has green eyes and brown hair, and at the time of her disappearance, she was 4 feet 10 inches tall and weighed 85 pounds. She was last seen wearing a light blue and white floral print shirt, blue and white shorts, and white sneakers. She was also wearing a silver Timex watch and a white gold class ring with a diamond. She had a purse with a horse or unicorn on it and was carrying a Roger Rabbit key ring. If you have any information about Tracy, please contact the Pennsylvania State Police at 717-362-8700.

JASON LANDRY

Jason Landry left his apartment in San Marco, Texas around 11:00 pm on Sunday, December 13, 2020. The 21-year-old, who was a student at Texas State University, had finished all his finals and was heading to his parents' home in Missouri City, Texas for winter break. He was in a good mood when he set out to make the 165-mile drive to Missouri City, but he never arrived at his parents' house. His Nissan Altima was found, wrecked and abandoned, later that night; it was just 30 miles away from his apartment. Jason wasn't anywhere near his car and he was never seen again.

A volunteer firefighter returning home after a call found the Altima on Salt Flat Road near Luling, Texas shortly after 12:30 am and called the police, telling them that the car had crashed into a tree. An officer with the Texas Highway Patrol responded to the scene of the crash but found no sign of Jason. Initially, the officer believed that they were likely dealing with a drunk driver who had crashed his car and then fled the scene to avoid getting arrested. He called for a tow truck to pick up the Altima and take it to an impound lot.

When the car was found, its headlights were on and the keys were still in the ignition. All the doors except for the front driver's side door were locked, and Jason's cell phone and some other personal belongings were found inside. Around 900 feet away from the car, the officer found Jason's backpack, a ball cap, a small bag of toiletries, and a plastic tumbler containing his beta fish, which were dead. Inside his backpack, the officer found a small amount of marijuana, Jason's laptop, and some gaming equipment.

While the officer was waiting for the tow truck to arrive, he went through the glove compartment and found the car's registration; it was registered to Jason's parents, Kent and Lisa Landry. The officer called and told them that the Altima had been in an accident; when they learned that Jason wasn't at the scene, Kent immediately drove to Luling to see what was going on. Kent, the senior pastor of a Missouri City church, was desperate to find his son and didn't feel that the Highway Patrol was doing enough to locate Jason. He decided to conduct his own search of the area.

Kent found several articles of Jason's clothing, including a pair of shorts, a shirt, a pair of socks, a pair of underwear, a pair of shoes, and a wristwatch. Interviews with Jason's friends at school later confirmed that the items of clothing found in the street were the same items he had been wearing when he left to make the drive home. This seemed to indicate that Jason had stripped out of his clothing after getting out of his wrecked car, despite the fact that the temperature was only a few degrees above freezing.

Investigators said that there was no evidence Jason's car had been forced off the road; all the damage to his car had been made when he impacted two trees after skidding off the road. It was possible he had swerved to avoid hitting a deer and then overcorrected, resulting in his car spinning around and slamming into the trees, hitting them trunk-first. There was no paint or other evidence to suggest a second vehicle had been involved.

By Monday night, state and local police departments, as well as dozens of volunteers, were involved in the search for Jason. Investigators believed that the crash had likely occurred shortly before it was discovered, meaning that Jason had only a limited amount of time to get out of the area before police arrived. They weren't sure if he had walked off on his own or had been picked up by someone, but no one came forward claiming to see him after the crash.

Texas Department of Public Safety Sgt. Deon Cockrell said that a handful of different agencies were assisting in the search, but by Tuesday night they still didn't know what had happened to Jason. "We have searched the entire area with DPS helicopters, drones…other agencies have come out, state and local…even the Texas search and rescue team with their canines." All came up empty.

Lisa Landry was worried that Jason had been injured in the crash and was unable to make his way home. "He's alone, he doesn't have his phone or his wallet, and it's cold outside…maybe he's hurt." A few drops of blood had been found on some of his clothing that had been left in the road, but it wasn't enough to suggest he was seriously injured.

Despite the fact that they hadn't found any indications that Jason was still in the area, Sgt. Cockrell said the search would continue. "We're going to keep on searching until we think there's no hope, which could be two days, three days, four days from now. We're going to keep on searching until we either find him or find an answer."

The search intensified on Tuesday, and Texas EquuSearch joined the hunt for Jason. Search teams combed through the remote area northeast of Luling where the car had been found. Felix Cortinas, who owned property in the area, told reporters, "It's a place where someone could easily get lost. A lot of old wells...old wells that were never even capped or cemented, just holes. And a lot of creeks, a lot of steep banks."

Tracking dogs were able to pick up Jason's scent leading away from the car, indicating that he had walked away from the accident. The dogs followed his scent toward Luling for about a quarter of a mile before it disappeared; it was possible he had gotten into a car with someone at that point.

The search continued on Wednesday, and officials decided to search a pond that was near the accident site after search dogs seemed to pick up Jason's scent near the edge of the water. The search team got a sonar hit that resembled the shape of a body, prompting the decision to drain the pond. Jason's family tried to prepare themselves for the worst and waited anxiously while the pond was drained. There was no sign of Jason.

The Texas Department of Safety and members of Texas EquuSearch spent Thursday going back over several areas near where Jason's car had been found, looking for anything that might have been missed in the initial search. They didn't come up with anything, and admitted that they were starting to fear the worst.

A reporter asked Kent if he thought Jason might be hiding somewhere, afraid to come home because he had wrecked his parent's car, but Kent didn't think that was the case. He did, however, have a message for Jason. "Don't worry about that...the car is just a stupid car. We love you. Call someone. Call the police. Come home. We just want you home."

A week after Jason went missing, there had been little progress made in locating him. A prayer vigil was held for the missing man on December 20, 2020, and his parents thanked the community for all of their support during the search effort. Kent noted, "We are living the worst dreams of every parent. It feels like a bad dream. A bad dream we've been hoping to wake up from...I pray my son is alive and pray that someone is taking care of him."

The Caldwell County Sheriff's Office wasn't immediately called to investigate Jason's disappearance as the Highway Patrol officer who responded to the car crash hadn't thought there was anything unusual about the accident. This meant that investigators from the sheriff's office never had a chance to look at the car before it was towed to an impound lot; Jason had been missing for nearly a week before the case was transferred to them. Caldwell County Sgt. William Miller admitted, "There were certain things that weren't done in the first hours after the discovery...we weren't conducting a true missing persons investigation." Once the case was handed over to the sheriff's office, they had to play catch-up. They were working to determine where Jason had been in the hours before the car crash and were interviewing his friends and classmates.

On December 22, 2020, volunteers with Texas EquuSearch said they would be suspending their search for Jason. They felt that the entire area had been thoroughly searched without finding any evidence of Jason; they assured Jason's family that they would launch another search if the sheriff's office developed any credible leads about where Jason might be.

Investigators combed through an additional 300 acres of land near Luling but didn't find any sign of Jason. They also used a drone to take video footage of the entire area, which was then painstakingly combed through for any potential evidence. As with all the other searches, however, they came up empty.

As the physical search for Jason drew to a close,

Caldwell County Sheriff Daniel Law felt confident that the missing man was not anywhere within the 31 square miles that had been searched. "We will not speculate on what may have happened to Jason, but we feel the vast area surrounding the accident scene has been thoroughly searched and Jason still hasn't been found."

Detectives from the Caldwell County Sheriff's Office traveled to Missouri City and interviewed Jason's parents and siblings; they also collected several things that had been found inside Jason's car so they could be processed for potential forensic evidence.

Kent made a public appeal for anyone with information about his son's whereabouts to come forward. "If someone knows something, [or] might know something, might have seen him...please tell someone." He was desperate to have his son home in time for Christmas.

Sgt. Miller told reporters that he didn't have enough information to form an opinion about what had happened to Jason, but he was still hoping to find him alive. "We are trying to run down all of our leads. It would have been easier if we had started a week ago." Jason's family agreed; they were very critical of the way the Texas Department of Public Safety had handled the case and wondered if Jason would have been found immediately had the case been assigned to the sheriff's office from the beginning.

On January 29, 2021, the Caldwell County Sheriff's Office stated that they had been able to gain access to most of Jason's cell phone and computer data. They learned that he briefly stopped using his GPS to open Snapchat on his phone at 11:24 pm on the night he vanished. He missed a turn and ended up on Salt Flat Road, where his car was found at 12:31 am. Although his cell phone was still on and had a signal, he never used it again after 11:24 pm, and officials were trying to determine what happened after that.

In a Facebook post, the sheriff's office wrote, "There is no evidence that Jason was traveling to meet with or had communicated intent to meet with anyone in or around Luling." They believed he had ended up on the isolated dirt road simply by accident after missing a turn he should have taken.

The Caldwell County Sheriff's Office and the Texas Rangers were working together to process evidence in the case; this included submitting several of the items for DNA testing to confirm that they belonged to Jason.

On February 26, 2021, Texas Search and Rescue conducted a three-day search for Jason. The group used dog teams, searchers on horseback, drones, and helicopters to scour Caldwell County. They covered around 50 square miles but unfortunately found no sign of Jason.

In May 2021, Jason's family announced that they were offering a $10,000 reward for information leading to his safe return. Tuleta Copeland, a retired FBI agent who volunteered to search for missing people, noted, "If you know anything or if you've seen anything, we can protect you…we can keep you confidential. Just call us and talk to us."

A year after Jason set out to drive home for the holidays, he was still missing. Although his case remained open, investigators hadn't been able to develop any substantial leads and still had no idea what had happened to him. Both the Caldwell County Sheriff's Office and Texas Search and Rescue had conducted several additional searches for the missing student but hadn't found any clues to his whereabouts.

Months went by and the case started to stall. By

December 2022, Jason had been missing for two years and investigators couldn't agree about what happened to him. While detectives with the Caldwell County Sheriff's Office believe that Jason walked away from the accident and vanished on his own, his parents and a retired FBI investigator think that he was the victim of a crime.

Kent thinks that the initial officer on the scene wrote Jason off the moment he found marijuana in his backpack. "It just feels like your child is discarded, because they treated everything with this investigation with such indifference." Kent pointed out that he was the one who found Jason's clothing in the road – after Jason's car had already been towed.

By the second anniversary of their son's disappearance, Kent and Lisa had resigned themselves to the fact that Jason was likely no longer alive, but they wanted to know what had happened to him and bring him home for a proper burial.

Abel Pena, a retired FBI agent who heads Project Absentis, a non-profit organization that helps the families of missing persons, said that he and his team of investigators believe that Jason met with foul play. "I think the biggest red flags for us were the clothes just being laid where they were placed...we all agreed it appeared like it was staged." He doesn't believe Jason was behind the wheel of the car when it crashed.

Caldwell County Sheriff's Capt. Jeff Ferry agrees that Jason is likely dead, but he doesn't believe that it was the result of a crime. He noted that Jason had messaged his friends about marijuana and other personal things that night. "When we look at the totality of things, it really paints a picture of almost an internal crisis that Jason is dealing with." He thinks that Jason fled on foot after crashing his car and they have just been unable to find his remains.

Jason's parents just want to find him, no matter what the reason behind his disappearance might be. Kent pointed out that law enforcement seemed to make their mind up immediately that Jason was just a college kid on drugs and thus put little effort into finding him. "They saw his clothes lying in the middle of the road and didn't even bother to pick them up. If you literally think there is some college student naked in 30-degree weather...shouldn't you at least search for him?"

For Jason's parents, siblings, friends, and other relatives, he will always be more than just another missing college student. They have done everything possible to raise awareness about Jason's disappearance and make sure that he isn't forgotten. They have held prayer vigils, organized searches, and raised reward money. They hold their breath every time an unidentified body is found. And they hold onto the memories of all the good times they shared with Jason, praying that they will one day be reunited with him.

Jason David Landry was just 21 years old when he went missing from Luling, Texas in December 2020. Jason was driving home to Missouri City, Texas from his apartment at Texas State University in San Marco when he vanished; the circumstances surrounding his disappearance are murky and investigators have been unable to determine exactly what happened to him that night. Jason has brown hair and brown eyes, and at the time of his disappearance, he was 6 feet 1 inch tall and weighed 170 pounds. Jason has a scar on his left ankle and one on the right side of his neck. If you have any information about Jason, please contact the Caldwell County Sheriff's Office at 512-398-6777.

CLAUDIA LAWRENCE

Claudia Lawrence planned to get up earlier than usual on Thursday, March 19, 2009. The 35-year-old had to be to work at 6:00 am and her car was in the shop, so she was going to walk to her job as a chef at the University of York's Goodricke College. Claudia spoke to her mother, Joan, on Wednesday night and told her that she was going to have to get up before 5:00 am to make the three-mile walk to the university. She never showed up for work in the morning, however, and when her boss tried to call her cell phone, she didn't answer.

Claudia, who had been working at the university for three years, was normally a reliable employee who never failed to show up for work. Although her absence was worrying, co-workers assumed she would soon rush in the door with a good explanation for where she had been. By the end of the day, there had still been no word from Claudia but her boss didn't call anyone from her family to let them know.

Claudia had plans to meet her best friend, Suzy Cooper, at a pub Thursday night. When she didn't show up, Suzy tried calling her but got no answer. Knowing she had to get up early that morning, Suzy assumed Claudia had simply fallen asleep when she got home from work and slept through their meeting time. It wasn't until the following morning, when she still hadn't heard from her best friend, that Suzy grew worried and decided to call Claudia's father.

Peter Lawrence told Suzy he last spoke to his

daughter Wednesday night. He knew she planned to walk to work and had offered to let her borrow his car but she declined, telling him the weather was nice and she didn't mind the walk. Before hanging up, Claudia arranged to meet her father for a drink Friday evening. He hadn't expected to hear from her on Thursday so had no idea she hadn't made it to work.

Peter and Suzy met at Claudia's home in the northeastern section of York and knocked on her door. When there was no answer, Peter used his key to unlock the door. He and Suzy cautiously made their way inside and called out for Claudia, but they were met with silence. Most of Claudia's belongings, including her handbag and wallet, were inside; the only things that were missing were her cell phone and a small bag she used to carry her white chef's uniform back and forth to work.

Claudia's apartment was neat and showed no signs of a struggle inside. Her bed was made and there were a couple of dishes in her kitchen sink. A silver necklace and ring Claudia always wore when she went out at night were sitting on her bedside table where she always left them when she headed to her job as a chef. It looked as if Claudia had eaten breakfast and then left for work as usual on Thursday morning but hadn't made it there. Fearing that something had happened to her while she was walking to the University of York, her father called the North Yorkshire Police and reported her missing.

Since Claudia was an adult, free to come and go as she pleased, the police weren't initially too concerned about the fact that she was missing. They tried to assure her father that she had likely decided to get away from things for a few days and would return soon. Peter was unconvinced, pointing out that her money, bank cards, and passport were found inside her home, making it unlikely that she had taken off on an unexpected holiday.

Claudia had never before gone away without letting her parents and friends know first, and they were certain she wasn't missing voluntarily. She enjoyed her job and had no history of depression or mental illness. Suzy was adamant that Claudia wasn't the type of person who would just disappear. "Everyone loves her and this is just a total mystery to us all. Nothing was amiss in any of the texts she sent to me on Wednesday...she was her usual upbeat, bubbly self. None of this makes any sense."

The North Yorkshire Police searched along the route Claudia would normally take to get to work but found no evidence of a hit-and-run or any other kind of accident. They also checked surveillance footage from a CCTV camera at the Melrosegate Post Office but were unable to find any footage of Claudia walking past the post office on Thursday morning. Although the post office was located along the most direct route from Claudia's house to the University of York, they couldn't rule out that she had walked on one of the side streets that had no CCTV cameras.

Claudia last used her cell phone around 9:00 pm Wednesday; she didn't respond to any text messages or calls Thursday morning, but phone records show that her cell phone remained on until Thursday afternoon. Investigators determined that her phone was turned off at 12:10 pm Thursday, more than 12 hours after anyone last heard from Claudia. Her phone was connected to the same cell phone tower near her home the entire time.

After several days went by without any sign of Claudia, investigators admitted that there was a possibility she had been abducted while walking to work Thursday morning as they could find no other reason for her disappearance. Everyone they interviewed told them it was out of character for Claudia to be out of contact with her loved ones; she frequently called and texted her parents and friends.

Claudia's parents, Peter and Joan, were divorced, but Claudia remained close with each of them. She had called them both the night before she went missing, and neither one of them sensed anything was wrong with her at the time. She arranged to meet her father for a drink on Friday evening, and she and her mother made plans to get together that Sunday for Mother's Day. Joan offered to pay for her daughter to take a taxi to work since her car was in the shop, but Claudia declined, saying that she didn't mind the walk.

Peter said both he and Joan were extremely worried about their daughter. "It's the not knowing that is really hard to take, and the fact that Claudia has never gone missing before...it really is completely out of character for her." While they both hoped that Claudia was safe, they were convinced that she had been abducted and feared the worst.

As far as Claudia's parents were aware, she had no plans to go out Wednesday night since she had to get up early Thursday morning. She was at home when she called her mother around 8:10 pm and Joan assumed she was in for the night. On March 26, 2009, however, detectives said it was possible that Claudia had met up with someone she knew Wednesday night and something happened to her then. They noted that her phone usage stopped shortly after she spoke with her mother; this was out of character for Claudia, whose friends said she treated her phone as another appendage. She was constantly calling and texting her friends; the fact that her phone went quiet early Wednesday night was a red flag to police.

North Yorkshire Police Det. Supt. Ray Galloway said

that although no evidence of foul play was found, investigators didn't believe that Claudia left voluntarily. "My professional judgment is that Claudia has probably come to harm. It is highly likely she went with someone she knew...she would not have got into a vehicle that she didn't know and she wouldn't have gone to meet somebody she didn't know."

Detectives made a public appeal for anyone with information about the case to contact them; they were especially interested in hearing from people who might know if Claudia had been seeing anyone or planned to meet someone the night before she vanished. Investigators also conducted several searches of the York area but were unable to find any clues to Claudia's whereabouts.

Claudia's loved ones launched a social media campaign to raise awareness about her disappearance. Within a few days, a page dedicated to finding Claudia had more than 10,000 followers. Members of the York City Football Club joined the search effort as well, distributing flyers with Claudia's photograph at their game on Saturday, March 28, 2009. Nick Bassett, the club's secretary, told reporters, "We are hoping it will jog someone's memory and bring up some evidence that will help to find Claudia."

On April 2, 2009, investigators announced that they were trying to identify a pick-up truck that had been seen outside of Claudia's home around 9:00 pm the night before she went missing. The truck was believed to be a Ford Ranger Thunder, and it was possible it belonged to someone who had visited Claudia after she spoke with her mother Wednesday night.

Two weeks later, detectives said they had received information that a couple had been seen arguing on the side of University Road around 6:10 am on the day Claudia disappeared. The witness did not provide a description of the vehicle, though they said the passenger side door was open and a man and a woman were standing next to the car. According to Det. Supt. Galloway, "The man and woman appeared to be in some form of altercation. It's a significant line of inquiry which we wish to pursue."

Five weeks after Claudia went missing, detectives admitted that they no longer believed she was alive and they were treating the case as a murder inquiry. Det. Supt. Galloway told reporters, "We have no proof of her death, however, we also have no proof of her life." Hoping to bring in some new leads, Crimestoppers announced that they were offering a £10,000 reward for information leading to Claudia's whereabouts.

Claudia's father made another public appeal for information 50 days after his daughter was last seen. He was certain there were people in the community who knew what happened to Claudia and he pleaded for them to come forward. Detectives had followed up on more than 1,000 tips in the weeks following Claudia's disappearance but none brought them any closer to finding the missing woman. They had searched over 1,200 properties, dredged sewers, and sent divers into rivers and ponds. All their searches came up empty.

Det. Supt. Galloway said investigators were following up on several sightings they believed might be relevant to Claudia's disappearance. The week before she vanished, two men had been seen outside her home. At least one of the men, and possibly both, were Asian. Neither had been identified. There were also reports of a man and woman seen outside her home three days after she was reported missing. It was unknown if they had anything to do with her case as they were never identified.

Although Claudia's relatives and friends said they didn't believe she was in any kind of secret relationship, detectives weren't so sure. In June 2009, Det. Supt. Galloway appealed for anyone who had been involved with Claudia to come forward "if they wanted to be handled in a discreet, confidential, and controlled manner." He said Claudia had been involved "in relationships of complexity and mystery" that she had kept hidden from those closest to her.

Claudia didn't have a computer and didn't use any dating agencies to meet men; investigators believed that she likely met people at her local pub. She lived just a few doors down from the Nag's Head pub and met her friends there frequently. Detectives thought it was possible she met some romantic interests there as well, and they hoped that anyone who had been involved with the missing woman – or who knew of someone involved with her – would contact the police. Det. Supt. Galloway noted, "My real concern is that they, by not coming forward, will be protecting the person or people who have brought her to harm."

Peter was clinging to the hope that Claudia could still be alive, saying that until he had proof that she had been killed, he was going to remain optimistic. "It makes me very angry indeed that there are people who know something and aren't saying anything." He desperately wanted to know what had happened to her and did everything he could to keep her case in the public eye. He said he had no problems with the way the police were handling the case, although he didn't agree that Claudia had been involved in any relationships that she kept secret from her family.

Rumors started to spread that Claudia was involved in a number of illicit affairs with married men. Some people claimed Claudia had dated 30 or 40 different men, any one of whom could have killed her. Others tried to defend her reputation, stating that these claims were absurd and had no factual basis. With Claudia unable to give her side of the story, the rumors kept spreading until it was impossible to tell fact from fiction. George Forman, the manager of the Nag's Head, said Claudia did date some men from the bar, but the number was nowhere near as high as some people claimed. Over the past five years, she had dated maybe a dozen men. Detectives spoke with all of them but couldn't connect any of them to her disappearance.

Jen King, one of Claudia's close friends, lived with her for nearly a year after breaking up with her boyfriend. She said that during that entire time, she didn't see Claudia bring any men home. "There were certainly not 30 or 40 men tramping through our door...even if she had the brass to sneak somebody in I would have known. The walls were paper thin."

In September 2009, investigators confirmed that the last text message Claudia received the night before she vanished was from a male friend in Cyprus. He sent her a message at 9:12 pm that Wednesday night, but she didn't reply. Detectives said Claudia knew several people on the island of Cyprus; she had visited there before and had even been offered several jobs on the island. They were in the process of tracking down her contacts in Cyprus, though they admitted that they weren't sure if they had anything to do with her disappearance.

In late September, a new tip led investigators to search the biology department at the University of York. It wasn't the first time they had conducted a search on university property – they had previously searched through construction sites on campus – and they didn't find anything related to Claudia's disappearance.

Claudia should have been celebrating her 36th birthday with friends and family on February 27, 2010. Instead, detectives were still trying to determine exactly what happened to her. A recent television appeal had brought in a few new tips, one of which investigators said provided a "potentially significant lead."

As the first anniversary of Claudia's disappearance approached, investigators released new CCTV images of her. Taken the day before she went missing, they showed Claudia leaving work around 2:00 pm and stopping to mail a letter before heading home. Investigators hadn't been able to determine who she mailed the letter to, so it was unclear if it was relevant to her case or not.

In August 2010, the investigation into Claudia's disappearance seemed to stall. Investigators had exhausted all available leads but were no closer to finding Claudia than they had been on the day she was reported missing. There had been no reported sightings of her and no evidence found to suggest she was dead. Most of the detectives who had been working on the case were pulled off of it and assigned to other cases, though Claudia's family vowed to keep up their own search for the missing woman.

There was little progress in the investigation over the next three years, but in October 2013, detectives announced that they were going to take a fresh look at the case. Claudia's home was searched again in the hopes that technological advances might turn up some new evidence that had been missed during the initial search.

Over the next several years, detectives arrested several different men suspected of being involved in Claudia's presumed murder, but each one was released after questioning as none could be linked to any crime.

These included a 59-year-old co-worker who occasionally gave Claudia rides to work, the landlord of The Acomb pub in York, and four different customers of The Nag's Head. All denied any wrongdoing.

The investigation into Claudia's disappearance is still open, though there have been no new leads in recent months. The last major search took place in September 2021, when police drained a lake in North Yorkshire and conducted a fingertip search of the lake bottom. Detectives remain convinced that Claudia was murdered but they have been unable to find her body and no one had been charged in her death.

Claudia Lawrence was 35 years old when she went missing from her home in Heworth, near York, England. She was a bubbly and happy woman who enjoyed her job as a chef and liked spending time with her friends and family. Her loved ones are certain that she wouldn't have voluntarily disappeared; although they hope to find her alive, detectives believe she was murdered. If you have any information about Claudia's disappearance, please contact the North Yorkshire Police at 101 (if in the UK) or +44 1904 933043 from abroad. You can also contact Crimestoppers at 0800 555 111 or visit crimestoppers-uk.org.

JUDY MARTINS

Judy Martins was excited about her plans for the upcoming Memorial Day weekend in 1978. The 22-year-old, who was a junior at Kent State University in Kent, Ohio, was going to be spending the weekend with two of her friends in New York. On Tuesday, May 23, 1978, Judy left her dorm room in Engleman Hall and visited with some friends who lived in Dunbar Hall. After visiting with her friends for a couple of hours, Judy left their dorm room around 2:30 am Wednesday to make the five-minute walk back to Engleman Hall. She never made it back to her room and she was never seen again.

Judy was a resident assistant for her dormitory; one of the perks that came with the position was a single room. Because of this, Judy had no roommate to raise the alarm when she didn't make it back to her dorm room and her disappearance initially went unnoticed. One of her friends reported her missing to campus police Thursday night, and officials didn't call Judy's parents until Friday afternoon.

Kent State police initially believed that Judy had gone off voluntarily and would likely return once the holiday weekend was over. Although they told Judy's family that they had searched the campus for the missing student, the extent of their search was unknown. Most of Judy's classmates had already left for the weekend and weren't around to be questioned.

Friends who had seen Judy in the hours leading up to her disappearance told police that she had been in a good mood when she left Dunbar Hall and had planned to go right back to her room. The friends had been celebrating the fact that the spring quarter was almost over, and Judy had pranked her friends by dressing up as a prostitute that night. She had still been wearing a curly red wig when she left to walk back to her room.

Judy was the oldest daughter of Arthur and Dolores Martins; she had a younger sister and a younger brother. She was a 1973 graduate of Avon Lake High School, and she enrolled at Ohio University the fall after her graduation. She spent two years there before deciding to take some time off from school; after moving back in with her parents for a couple of years, she decided to go to Kent State.

Judy had always been a good student and was serious about her education. She was an art major at Kent State and was minoring in women's studies; she was hoping to one day become a therapist and hadn't ruled out the idea of going to graduate school. She enjoyed helping people and was a volunteer counselor at Kent State's Pregnancy Information Center.

A friendly and outgoing young woman, Judy made friends easily and was popular on campus. She loved to have fun and joke around with her friends; she was described as being the life of the party and could light up a room with her smile.

Although campus police insisted that Judy would return when she was ready, her family was adamant that Judy wasn't the type of person who would go anywhere for an extended amount of time without letting them know where she was going to be. Judy was especially close with her younger sister, Nancy; the two spoke on the phone frequently and Nancy was certain Judy would have called her if she were able.

From the beginning, the Kent police force seemed to want to downplay Judy's disappearance; her family believes the university was still trying to overcome the public relations nightmare caused by the Kent State shootings in 1970 and didn't want any negative press resulting from a missing student.

A week after Judy was last seen, officials with the Kent State University Police Department made a public appeal for information about Judy's whereabouts. They noted that the missing woman was "reliable and dependable" and her family didn't think she had vanished voluntarily. They said that they had contacted local police departments and listed Judy as missing with a nationwide police network, but they didn't have any organized searches planned.

The following week, Kent State Police Chief Robert Malone said that detectives had reason to believe that Judy had gone to Mexico. According to Chief Malone, Judy had been spotted at a Kent garage sale on Memorial Day; she had spent about an hour looking through the various items for sale before purchasing some clothing and told several residents that she was planning to hitchhike to Mexico. The witnesses were shown photographs of Judy and told investigators that they were certain she was the woman they had seen.

Although investigators believed that the witnesses were credible, Chief Malone told reporters that they were still going to conduct an aerial search of the Kent State campus and surrounding area. In addition, the Kent State University Foundation was offering a $1,500 reward for information leading to Judy's whereabouts.

Judy's parents didn't believe that she would have hitchhiked anywhere; she had no history of doing so and had her own car waiting for her at home. They believed it was most likely a case of mistaken identity and that the witnesses had actually seen someone else.

On June 5, 1978, the woman who had been seen at the garage sale was spotted again; this time she was getting a passport photograph taken in preparation for her trip to Mexico. Although she did resemble Judy, investigators spoke with her and were able to confirm she was not the missing woman. As Judy's parents had feared, the witnesses had been mistaken and their daughter's location remained a mystery.

Dolores was certain that her daughter hadn't planned to disappear. "We never had any problems with Judy. We always had a good relationship." All of Judy's belongings had been left behind in her dorm room, including her clothing, books, cosmetics, and eyeglasses. "I know every item of clothing she had. Nothing was missing" Judy had been wearing her contacts when she went missing; she never wore them overnight and likely intended to take them out as soon as she got back to her room. She had problems with her eyesight due to a flattened cornea, and she never would have traveled anywhere without taking her glasses with her.

Kent State officials admitted that they had no idea what had happened to Judy. They had used a helicopter equipped with heat-seeking radar to search the campus and a large wooded area but hadn't found any sign of Judy. All of Judy's friends and acquaintances were interviewed, and four people – including a man Judy had been dating – took and passed polygraph examinations. None of them were able to offer any clues as to what had happened to her.

Kent State Detective Tim Brandon was assigned Judy's case, but he told reporters that he didn't have a lot to work with. "We are investigating minor leads, but nothing has turned out to be significant." Her case failed to attract any meaningful media attention and as a result, detectives received few tips. Before the summer was over, the investigation had stalled and the case soon went cold.

In January 1980, Nan Abdo, a friend of the Martins family, announced that she was offering a $10,000 reward for information leading to Judy's return. "My father left me a small inheritance, so I wanted to do something concrete to help find Judy. It's a long shot, but maybe this will do the trick."

Judy's parents had considered hiring a private investigator to help locate their daughter, but they hadn't been able to afford one. Dolores noted, "They are out of the reach of the average family." They had been grateful when Nan decided to offer a reward for information and were hopeful that someone would finally come forward. "Somebody somewhere has to know something about where she is."

Although investigators with the Kent State Police Department said they were still actively working the case, they hadn't received any new tips in months. The lack of information had been hard on Judy's family. Dolores noted, "We've had some bizarre rumors from time to time, but they have led nowhere." One persistent rumor had been that Judy was working as a prostitute in Cleveland, Ohio. "We checked it out…it's unfounded."

Every week, Dolores would call investigators to see if there were any updates on Judy's case. Unfortunately, detectives never had anything new to report. "Some days are hard to get through. I would prefer to think that she's alive somewhere, but that's hard to believe now. She was so family oriented…I know she would have tried to at least call us."

Chief Malone admitted that the case had been a

frustrating one for detectives. "To my knowledge, this is the only case we have had at Kent State of a missing person who could not be accounted for...we get a lot of missing person reports here, but there always seems to be an explanation." Only Judy's case remained unexplainable.

In February 1980, Kent State Deputy Chief John Peach said detectives were looking into the possibility that a man named William Posey might have been involved in Judy's disappearance. Posey had been arrested and charged with the abduction and murder of a woman in Illinois, and Kent detectives became interested in him when they learned that he had lived in Kent from June 1978 until September 1979. There was no evidence linking him to Judy, however, and he denied having anything to do with her disappearance.

In March, Deputy Chief Peach told reporters that he didn't believe Posey had been responsible for Judy's disappearance. "We have placed him in Columbus on May 11, 1978, but we can't place him in Kent at all during May 1978."

Later that year, Posey pleaded guilty to murder charges in Illinois, and in 1981 he was convicted of kidnapping a woman in Vermont. He was sentenced to life in prison; in 2008, after being diagnosed with a terminal illness, he admitted that he had killed his Vermont kidnapping victim and told police he had thrown her body over a guardrail along Interstate 89 outside of Burlington. Posey was never charged in connection with Judy's case and always maintained that he had nothing to do with her disappearance.

Desperate to find their daughter, Arthur and Dolores decided to speak with a psychic. Although neither of them had ever believed in mediums before, they were willing to try anything. Dolores noted, "We brought this woman an article of Judy's clothing, and she told us things about Judy, personal things about her that were never in any newspaper, things that only we could know."

Unfortunately, the psychic didn't have good news for the couple. She told them that their daughter had been abducted and murdered by a trio of men. "She said Judy's body was ditched from an airplane flying at a low altitude. She said the body is in a heavily wooded, uninhabited island at least 50 miles northwest of Kent."

Police admitted that there were islands in Lake Erie that fit the description provided by the psychic, and officials assured the Martins that they would conduct a search of some of the islands once the weather got warmer. The psychic seemed to think they would be successful; she told Judy's parents, "The earth will give up Judy's body in April or May." By the end of May, it was clear that the psychic's prediction about Judy's recovery was wrong. She remained missing, and her case soon went cold once more.

Sadly, Judy's case appeared to be forgotten over the next several decades; there were no articles or news reports about the case and it was unclear if any detectives were still searching for her. Incredibly, in 2000, Kent University got rid of all its files concerning Judy's disappearance; officials apparently didn't see any need to keep the case active despite the fact that Judy had never been found. They later told Judy's family that the files had been properly disposed of in accordance with the university's records retention policy.

Deputy Chief Peach admitted that many of the records had been thrown away, but some had been shared with the Ohio Bureau of Criminal Investigation. "It was never classified as a crime, and that was before the guidelines for missing persons were established, well before we were able to keep electronic versions of records." He said that he still wondered what had happened to Judy so many years earlier. "It's just a bizarre case. To this day, it's too bizarre for me to even think what happened. We don't know it's a crime, but it's too unusual to think that a crime wasn't involved."

In the years since Judy went missing, both of her parents have died. Her sister, Nancy, noted that Judy's disappearance had deeply affected her mother and father. "Their lives were cut short by this." Arnold was just 57 when he died; Dolores was 71.

Nancy and her brother, Steve, submitted samples of their DNA to the Ohio Bureau of Criminal Investigation so they could build a profile for Judy and check for matches with unidentified bodies across the United States. Both siblings had come to terms with the fact that Judy is almost certainly dead, but they still wanted to be able to give her a proper burial. Steve noted, "The not knowing is very difficult, and it would be much better to know what happened, no matter how tragic."

For Nancy, one of the greatest tragedies is the fact that the Kent University Police Department didn't seem to care that her sister was missing. "That Kent State destroyed its files on Judy's disappearance is probably the most painful part." In May 2023, she noted, "We're at the point where we don't care about prosecution or anything else. All we want to know is where she is and what happened to her."

Judy Martins was just 22 years old when she vanished from Kent, Ohio in May 1978. Detectives initially believed that Judy had voluntarily gone missing, but her family was certain that she had been a victim of foul play. By the time investigators realized that Judy

wasn't a runaway, the case had already gone cold. Judy has hazel eyes and black hair, and at the time of her disappearance, she was 5 feet 4 inches tall and weighed 120 pounds. Judy was last seen wearing denim gaucho-style pants, a yellow and brown blouse, brown boots, and a light-colored trench coat. She was also wearing a curly red wig and carrying a large white purse. If you have any information about Judy, please contact the Ohio Attorney General's Office at 330-672-3070 or the U.S. Marshals Tip Line at 866-492-6833. You may remain anonymous.

SHIRLEY MCBRIDE

Shirley McBride left her sister's home in Concord, New Hampshire around 9:00 pm on Friday, July 13, 1984. The 15-year-old – known as Tippy to family and friends – planned to stop by the home of a woman whose children she babysat to pick up the money she was owed for her last babysitting job. Tippy told her sister, Donna Whitcomb, that she was going to stop by to visit her boyfriend at his workplace after she picked up her money. She expected to return to her sister's house in a couple of hours, but she never made it back and she was never seen again.

When Tippy failed to return home that night, Donna called her parents, Jack and Shirley McBride, and asked if they had seen the teenager. They hadn't heard from Tippy, and neither had any of her friends. The following day, they called the Concord Police Department and reported Tippy missing. Since Tippy had a history of running away from home, the police felt she had likely done so again and would show up in a few days.

Tippy had lived in Manchester, New Hampshire with her parents until September 1983, when the family moved to Pittsfield, New Hampshire. Jack and Shirley had viewed the move as a positive one – they had the chance to buy some land there and wanted more room for their five children – but Tippy hadn't been happy about leaving Manchester.

Tippy started acting out after the move; she began smoking marijuana and frequently skipped school. She would often hitchhike to Concord so she could visit her sister, and she begged her parents to let her live with Donna, who was 24 years old at the time. Jack said that they weren't thrilled about the idea, but eventually allowed Tippy to move to Concord. "We let her stay because she's just starting to feel her oats. We couldn't fight her."

Donna told reporters that Tippy had enjoyed living in Concord, and she hadn't given any indication that she was thinking about running away. "She liked it over here, she had a lot of freedom. She and I were very close – she told me everything...it's not like she was mad or anything before she left."

Jack and Shirley had visited their daughter the day before she went missing. They had taken her shopping and bought her some new summer clothes. There had been no indication anything was wrong at that time; Tippy seemed happy to be living with Donna and was pleased with her new clothes. She didn't take any extra clothing with her when she vanished, leading her parents to believe that she had intended to return.

Fearing that police weren't going to do much to locate Tippy, her family launched their own search for her. They went to all the usual teen hangouts in Concord, but no one they spoke with had any idea where Tippy might be. After several weeks went by with no word from Tippy, her parents started to worry that she hadn't left voluntarily. Jack pointed out, "We've always known where she was...she's always been in touch. I just can't see her leaving without being in contact with someone."

After Tippy picked up her babysitting money, she had planned to go to Concord Litho where her boyfriend worked. Her boyfriend – who was 21 years old at the time – was initially considered a possible suspect in the 15-year-old's disappearance, but detectives were unable to find any evidence to suggest that Tippy made it to his work that night. It appeared that she went missing before she was able to make it that far.

Later, Tippy's parents learned that Tippy and her boyfriend had been having problems; according to some of the teenager's friends, the boyfriend had dumped Tippy and she had been angry with him. Some believed that she was heading to his workplace not to meet up with him, but because she wanted to pour sugar into the gas tank of his prized motorcycle.

Three weeks after Tippy was last seen, her parents were at Donna's apartment when a man knocked on the door and said he thought he had just seen Tippy in downtown Concord. He agreed to take Donna to where he saw the teenager, and at first, she thought the girl was her missing sister. She looked just like Tippy, but it wasn't her.

Concord Police Lt. Paul Murphy said there were some red flags that made detectives fear that Tippy might have been a victim of foul play. "Tippy unfortunately hung out with some tough kids. She had some good friends, but she had some tough friends – friends that were known to law enforcement." He noted that Tippy would sometimes go with Donna to visit people who were incarcerated at the state prison; he didn't think this was an appropriate activity for a 15-year-old.

Lt. Murphy was also concerned by the fact that Tippy hadn't taken any of her belongings with her when she left home. "She left behind everything that a person would normally take if they were going to run away. So right away you have the impression it might not have been her idea to leave."

Investigators interviewed Tippy's friends and relatives but were unable to determine what had happened to the missing teenager. Jack told reporters that he believed detectives were doing everything they could to find his daughter but the lack of information was frustrating. "They get a story here, they get a story there...everything is different. But they know as little now as when they started."

Detectives spoke with Tippy's friends and associates in Concord, Manchester, and Pittsfield. There were several reported sightings of the teenager in the Manchester area, but when investigators followed up on the sightings they were unable to confirm any of them.

The holiday season came and went without any progress in the case. Tippy's parents wanted to believe that she had run away from home and would return safely, but as more time passed they started to worry that something had happened to Tippy. They were certain that she would have called someone if she were able to, but no one had heard from her since she went missing.

In January 1985, Tippy's parents announced that they were offering a $1,000 reward for information leading to their daughter's whereabouts. Jack told reporters that the family and police had been looking for Tippy daily but hadn't made any progress in locating her. "We're trying every avenue...she's been missing for almost seven months. The police have already questioned everything that came up...they have questioned everybody. The police have been doing all they can do."

Jack and Shirley had taken photographs of Tippy to hospitals throughout the state, hoping that one of them might recognize the teenager. Jack drove from their home in Pittsfield to Concord several times a week to search for Tippy, spending hours sitting outside video arcades and other places where teenagers liked to hang out. He admitted he and Shirley had even consulted several psychics but none had been able to tell them where to find their daughter. "It's tough not knowing anything."

Concord Police Sgt. John Clark had the unenviable task of reviewing daily teletypes containing descriptions of unidentified bodies found across the country. He hadn't come across any that matched Tippy's description. "It's frustrating. So many people have been talked to…potential leads have all been cleared and found to lead nowhere."

Detectives interviewed the prisoners who Tippy and Donna had visited. A couple of the men they visited had been released from prison, and investigators tracked them down and interviewed them as well. None of them were able to provide any leads.

In June 1985, Shirley's father – Tippy's grandfather – died after a brief illness. The family hoped that Tippy might see the news in the local paper and return home for the funeral, but there was no word from her.

As the first anniversary of Tippy's disappearance approached, investigators developed their first solid suspect. They had received a tip that Walter Davis, a 26-year-old who lived in Merrimack, New Hampshire, had exhibited suspicious behavior around the time that Tippy vanished. His mother and sister found him trying to burn some clothing in their fireplace despite the fact that it was July. They took the clothing away from him before he could light it on fire and asked him where he had gotten it. He claimed he had raped a girl and thrown her into a river.

Walter's sister showed the clothing to Stacie Coburn, one of her friends. Stacie was horrified when she learned the backstory of how Walter got the clothing; she immediately called her mother and asked her to come pick her up. Stacie and her mom then went to the Merrimack Police Department and told officers there about Walter's confession. Detectives went to Walter's home and collected the clothing as potential evidence.

Investigators showed the clothing – bib overalls and a cotton T-shirt – to Jack and Shirley, and they agreed that the clothing likely belonged to their daughter. When detectives interviewed Walter, however, he denied saying that he had raped the owner of the clothing. Instead, he claimed he had found the clothes in White Park Pond and brought them home because he thought they might fit his sister. He didn't explain why he had been caught trying to burn the items.

Investigators scoured the park, pond, the Merrimack River, and Walter's property for any sign of Tippy but found nothing. Cadaver dogs were brought in to see if they could pick up on anything, but they didn't alert anywhere. With no body – and no way to prove with certainty that the clothing had belonged to Tippy – detectives didn't have the evidence necessary to arrest Walter and no charges were filed.

Months turned into years, and investigators still had no idea what had happened to Tippy. Bruce Russell, who had been the director of investigations for the Concord Police for nearly three decades, retired in September 1987. He told reporters that Tippy's case was one of the unsolved cases that troubled him the most. "There are so many unanswered questions. No one knows whether she ran away or was kidnapped, whether she is alive or dead...she walked downtown one night and was never heard from again."

In November 1989, Jack announced that he was willing to pay a $5,000 reward to anyone with information leading to Tippy's location, alive or dead. He was desperate to find out what had happened to her, and said that the increased reward would only be available for 90 days. He hoped the time limit would encourage someone to finally come forward with the information needed for detectives to close the case. Sadly, if anyone knew where Tippy was, they remained silent.

By 1991, Tippy had been missing for seven years and detectives still had no idea what had happened to her. Sgt. Clark admitted her disappearance was "one of those great missing person tales…it's like someone picked them up in a spaceship and flew them away." He had left the Concord Police Department in 1986 but found he was unable to forget about Tippy. "In all my years of police work, the one thing I still constantly think about is whatever happened to Tippy McBride."

Sgt. Murphy acknowledged that Tippy had engaged in risky behavior and this had complicated the investigation. "One of the problems was Tippy would thumb and get into a car with anybody. The fact that she would hitchhike adds a whole new dimension to this." Detectives learned that she had once hitched a ride with someone who had an extensive criminal background and had developed a friendship with him; investigators interviewed him several times but found nothing to suggest that he was involved in the teen's disappearance.

Detectives received sporadic tips over the years and followed up on each one. They had checked shopping malls, strip clubs, hospitals, and morgues. Sgt. Murphy noted that they had found no trace of Tippy. "In the long run, I don't know that we're much closer today than we were four or five months after the investigation started."

Jack and Shirley refused to give up on the hope that their daughter was still alive, but in their hearts, they seemed to accept the fact that she had likely been a victim of foul play. Jack admitted, "Right at the start I knew something had happened, but I still have hope."

By March 1996, Jack and Shirley had lost all hope of

finding Tippy alive; they decided it was time to have their daughter legally declared dead. It was merely a formality; Jack stated that they wanted to be able to stop paying Tippy's life insurance and collect on the policy. He knew that it wouldn't bring the family any closure. "That'll only happen if her body is found."

Shirley died in October 2003 without ever learning what had happened to her daughter. Jack vowed to continue his fight for justice, but detectives admitted that they hadn't had any new leads in years. In 2008, investigators took a fresh look at the case, hoping to find something that had been missed during the initial investigation. The case was also featured on an episode of the Fox 25 television show, "New England's Most Wanted."

Concord Police Detective Todd Flanagan told reporters that he believed Tippy had been killed, but admitted that he didn't have enough evidence to prove it. "We have developed information that she never left Concord and may in fact have met with foul play that night." Although the name of Tippy's boyfriend has never been released publicly, detectives still considered him a person of interest in the case. Walter Davis remained the prime suspect, but he died in 2005, taking any secrets he might have had to his grave.

In 2014, investigators submitted the clothing found in Walter's possession for advanced DNA testing, but they were unable to retrieve any useable evidence. Despite the setback, detectives still believe the case can be solved and they continue to search for Tippy.

Shirley Ann McBride was just 15 years old when she vanished from Concord, New Hampshire in July 1984. She was a free-spirited teenager who longed to be an

independent adult and hung out with friends who were older than she was. Detectives believe she was likely murdered, but her body was never found. Tippy has blue eyes and brown hair, and at the time of her disappearance, she was 5 feet 6 inches tall and weighed 110 pounds. If you have any information about Tippy, please contact the Concord Police Department at 603-225-8600.

WESLEY MORGAN

Wesley Morgan was playing with four puppies in his Bluff Creek, Louisiana front yard on the morning of Tuesday, May 15, 2001. The 2-year-old was left unsupervised for a few minutes around 9:45 am, when his mother, 19-year-old Ruby Havard, went inside to boil some eggs. When she came back outside a few minutes later, Wesley and two of the puppies were missing. After briefly searching for him on her own, Ruby called the East Feliciana Parish Sheriff's Office and reported Wesley missing.
    Officials immediately launched a large-scale search for the missing toddler. Dozens of deputies, firefighters, and volunteers combed through the wooded area surrounding Wesley's home on Louisiana Highway 63. One of the missing puppies was found on the opposite side of Highway 63; the puppy was found some distance from the home and deputies said they didn't believe that a 2-year-old would have wandered that far.
    As hours went by without any sign of the missing toddler, police brought in bloodhounds, horses, ATVs, and a helicopter to assist in the search. Firefighters used a portable pump to drain a small pond near the home; they were soon able to rule out the possibility that Wesley had fallen into the water. Deputies searched through a nearby creek and Sheriff Talmadge Bunch dove into a second pond located across the street from where Wesley was last seen. They found nothing to indicate that Wesley was in the area.

On Wednesday, officials with the East Feliciana Parish Sheriff's Office requested the assistance of the FBI. Although they hadn't found any evidence to suggest that Wesley had been a victim of foul play, they couldn't eliminate the possibility. Agents spent several hours searching through the home Wesley shared with his mother and her boyfriend, 37-year-old Burnell Hilton; they also searched Burnell's pickup truck.

On Wednesday afternoon, detectives questioned Ruby, Burnell, and Wesley's father, Dewey Morgan, but they told reporters that they didn't learn anything that brought them any closer to finding Wesley. Dewey, who had volunteered in the search for his missing son, admitted that he feared the little boy had been kidnapped; he didn't think the toddler would have strayed far from his front yard and was concerned by the fact that he hadn't yet been located.

A Louisiana National Guard helicopter with thermal imaging equipment conducted several aerial searches of the area on Wednesday night but found no evidence that Wesley was anywhere near his home. Thursday morning, investigators used a cadaver dog to search several parts of East Feliciana Parish; the dog was unable to find any trace of Wesley.

Two days after Wesley was last seen, Chief Deputy Sheriff Paul Perkins admitted that detectives believed Wesley had been either kidnapped or murdered. What had started as a routine missing person case had turned into a criminal investigation.

FBI agents focused their attention on the adults closest to Wesley; on Thursday, they administered polygraph examinations to Ruby, Burnell, and Burnell's 17-year-old son. Burnell told reporters that Ruby wasn't dealing well with the situation. "They've been treating us like murderers. They're looking at the wrong people. But, like they said, they're doing their job."

On Friday, officials announced that Burnell had been arrested on charges unrelated to Wesley's disappearance. He was accused of shooting a Zachary, Louisiana man in the face during an argument in October 1998; he was arrested for attempted second-degree murder.

Investigators widened their search for Wesley over the weekend. A large portion of East Feliciana Parish was searched on foot, horseback, and ATVs. Volunteers drove along all the backroads in the parish, checking culverts and driveways for any clues to Wesley's whereabouts. Bluff Creek Assistant Fire Chief Darryl Buhler admitted that people were starting to get discouraged. "Now we're looking for a kid down on the ground, unconscious or something else. Right now, we're frustrated. Everybody's tired and emotionally drained."

Hundreds of volunteers participated in the search for Wesley; residents donated food and coffee for the search teams. Members of the close-knit community were stunned by the toddler's disappearance and wanted to do anything they could to help bring him home.

Sheriff Bunch believed that those closest to Wesley knew more about his disappearance than they were admitting. "As deep in my heart as I can believe, that baby never left that house walking...he was carried out of there." He was certain that Ruby and Burnell had done something to the toddler. "Both of them failed their polygraphs. They know something about this...his was off the charts."

Although the sheriff believed that Ruby and Burnell were responsible for Wesley's disappearance, he didn't necessarily believe that they had killed him. He noted that the National Guard was confident Wesley's body wasn't in the area. "They told me they would have picked him up with their equipment even if he was buried two feet under the ground." Sheriff Bunch thought it was more likely that Ruby had decided to sell or arrange for the illegal adoption of her son. "I'm praying and hoping that we can get this baby back alive."

Sheriff Bunch appealed to the public for help in determining what had happened to Wesley. "We've gotten to the point that Ruby won't talk to us...but somewhere down the line, she's got to put her trust in somebody and that person could help us."

Three weeks after Wesley was reported missing, the East Feliciana Parish Sheriff's Office conducted another search for him after consulting with a psychic who believed the little boy had been buried near a creek in Clinton, Louisiana. Investigators used a cadaver dog to search the area pinpointed by the psychic but came up empty. Sheriff Bunch admitted that it had been a long shot but he was desperate to find the missing toddler. "I may be crazy, but at this point, I'll try anything."

A couple of weeks after Burnell was arrested, Ruby apparently decided it was time to move on from him. She started dating a man who lived in East Baton Rouge Parish, and detectives searched his home after receiving reports that a toddler had been seen there. The man wasn't able to provide them with any useful information about the case and investigators found nothing to indicate that Wesley had ever been at his home.

Sadly, by the time Wesley had been missing for a month, his case had completely faded from the headlines. Although investigators continued searching for the toddler, they didn't believe Ruby was telling them the truth about what happened but were unable to prove otherwise. The case soon stalled and then went cold.

In December 2015, retired Baton Rouge police officer Richard Sobers spent a day standing in front of the East Feliciana Parish courthouse to raise awareness about Wesley's case. Richard handed out missing person flyers and bumper stickers asking, "Where's Wesley?" The retired officer noted that Wesley's family had never seemed interested in finding the missing boy, and he didn't think officials were doing enough to solve the case. "I don't understand why people are not looking for him."

Sheriff Bunch still believed that Ruby had been directly involved in her son's disappearance and had most likely sold the toddler. "I know he's alive somewhere." In 2008, a pregnant Ruby had been charged with attempting to sell her unborn child to a married couple for several thousand dollars. The sale didn't go through and the charges were eventually dropped, but investigators thought it was likely that Wesley hadn't been as lucky.

Rhonda Covington, the public defender who had represented Ruby when she was charged in 2008, denied that she knew what had happened to Wesley. She claimed that Ruby was still hopeful that she would one day be reunited with her missing son, but detectives pointed out that Ruby hadn't checked on the status of his case since shortly after he was reported missing. Perhaps most telling, Ruby and the rest of her family were not supportive of Richard Sobers and his efforts to help find Wesley.

In 2016, the FBI announced that they were reopening their investigation into Wesley's disappearance. More than 20 billboards with information about the case were placed throughout Louisiana and Mississippi; the billboards included an age-progression photograph of what Wesley might look like as a teenager. Investigators hoped that the billboards would bring in some new tips and help them finally determine what had happened to the little boy. The agency also announced that they were offering a $10,000 reward for information leading to Wesley's recovery.

Wesley's paternal aunt, Mary Dufour, was pleased to learn that his case was being reopened. "I just hope and pray he hasn't been abused...you just hope and pray for the best." She noted that Wesley would be turning 18 the following year and she hoped he would be home with his family to celebrate his birthday.

Although the billboards helped generate a number of tips, none of them led investigators to Wesley and his case quickly went cold once more. Detectives continue to follow up on each lead they receive, but there has been no movement on the case in years. Some detectives believe that Wesley is still alive and simply unaware of his past but may have hazy memories of a childhood in rural Louisiana.

Ruby continues to maintain that Wesley wandered away from home while she was inside cooking eggs; although investigators believe this is the least-likely scenario, if Wesley did wander away it's possible he was abducted by a stranger or he might have succumbed to the elements. Searchers combed through a five-mile area surrounding Wesley's house and found no sign of the toddler; if he did walk away, he did so without leaving any footprints behind.

Wesley Dale Morgan was just 2 years old when he went missing from the Bluff Creek community in Clinton, Louisiana in May 2001. The circumstances surrounding his disappearance are unclear and detectives do not believe he wandered away from his home. Wesley has blue eyes and blond hair, and at the time of his

disappearance, he was 3 feet tall and weighed 40 pounds. Wesley was last seen wearing blue shorts, a gray Mickey Mouse T-shirt, and a pair of sandals. If you have any information about Wesley, please contact the East Feliciana Parish Sheriff's Office at 225-683-5459.

DENISE PFLUM

Denise Pflum left her Everton, Indiana home around 12:30 pm on Friday, March 28, 1986. The 18-year-old, who was on spring break from Connersville High School that week, had gone to a party the previous night and realized when she got home that she had left her purse at the party. She made a few phone calls to friends to see if anyone wanted to go with her to retrieve it, but none of her friends were available so she told her parents, David and Judith, that she was going to go by herself. She climbed into her 1981 Buick Regal and drove off. She was never seen again.

The party Denise had attended Thursday night had been held outdoors on some local farmland, but it doesn't appear that Denise ever made it there on Friday. A farmer working in a field in Glenwood, Indiana, approximately three miles away from where the party was held, saw her light-colored Buick parked on his farm Friday afternoon around 1:00 pm, but he never saw its driver. He assumed that the car belonged to someone who was hunting for mushrooms, a common activity in the area. He grew suspicious when it was still parked there on Saturday and called the Fayette County Sheriff's Department to report it.

Deputies quickly determined that the car was associated with a missing person report and treated it as a crime scene. The car was locked and there were no signs of a struggle inside or around it. Hoping to find some clues to Denise's whereabouts, police conducted a large-scale search of the area surrounding where the car was located. Searchers on foot, horseback, and in a plane scoured the area but found no sign of the missing teenager.

Denise's car had been found about a half-mile away from Route 44, close to the Rush-Fayette county line. David and Judith told investigators that they didn't believe Denise knew anyone who lived in that area and they had no idea why she would have driven there. Fayette County Detective Ted McQuinley told reporters that Denise's car was devoid of clues. "There was nothing inside. It was like she drove the car into the lane and parked, got out, locked it up, and vanished."

Fayette County Sheriff George Zimmerman told reporters that Denise had no history of running away and it was out of character for her to go anywhere without letting her parents know. "She's a straight-A honor roll student. She's the type of person who doesn't do this type of thing." She didn't take any of her belongings with her; her missing purse was later found at the property where the party had been held.

Denise was a senior at Connersville High School and had been looking forward to graduating in a few months. She had excellent grades – she had been accepted to Miami University in Oxford, Ohio – and she was a great athlete. She was on the basketball team and the track team at her high school and was one of the top students in her class.

On Wednesday, April 2, 1986, around 100 police officers and firefighters scoured through the 100-acre plot of land in rural Fayette County where the party had been held the previous week. They found no clues to Denise's whereabouts there, so the search was shifted to the location where her car had been found. Searchers combed through more than 300 acres of land there, but once again came up empty.

Detective McQuinley admitted that the lack of clues was frustrating. "It was a tremendous effort...at this point, we have searched everything that we had any kind of information on that needs to be searched at this time."

A week after Denise was last seen, there had been little progress in determining what had happened to her. Detectives told reporters that they had eliminated the possibility that the teenager was a runaway; despite the lack of clues, they were convinced that foul play was involved in her disappearance.

Detective McQuinley told reporters that Denise's family was focused on finding her alive. "They're holding up much better than might be expected...I think that faith is holding them together. They just have to have faith, knowing their daughter's character and that law enforcement is doing all it can...keep hoping, that's about all they can do."

David and Judith hadn't returned to work since their daughter went missing. Judith told reporters that they were trying to remain positive. "We are not convinced that she ran away, but we hope that's what happened; the alternatives are not good...a nightmare is the best way to describe it."

Neither parent had noticed any sort of change in Denise's behavior before she vanished; her mother stated that the teenager had been her usual friendly and cheerful self in the weeks leading up to her disappearance. Denise and her boyfriend had recently broken up, but it had been a mutual decision and they were still great friends. Her former boyfriend had been in contact with police and Judith didn't believe he had any involvement in Denise's disappearance.

A spokesperson for the Indiana State Police

admitted that they hadn't uncovered any clues to Denise's location. "The investigation remains at square one." He said that detectives were continuing to classify Denise as a missing person; they didn't believe she had voluntarily disappeared, but they hadn't found any solid evidence to suggest she had been killed.

On April 7, 1986, detectives asked people in Lawrence County, Indiana to keep an eye out for Denise. Although they stressed that they still didn't believe the teenager was a runaway, they noted that she knew a number of people in Lawrence County through various sports meets. Indiana State Police Detective Sgt. Claude Trent told reporters that they hadn't received any tips that Denise was in the area. "We're just covering all the bases."

Detective McQuinley told reporters that he had a personal stake in finding Denise; her father was his cousin. "I don't care who finds her, as long as she's found. We'd just like to see her back home safe." He noted that all missing person cases bothered him, but this one even more so than usual. "When it's someone in the family, it adds a little pressure."

He stated that investigators had received a few tips about potential sightings of Denise, but none of them could be confirmed. "There were some possible sightings up around Indianapolis from people who didn't know her...you just can't get your hopes up too high on something like that." Detectives followed up on each tip but none led them to Denise.

Investigators combed through Denise's address book and contacted each person listed in it. None of them were able to provide any clues about what might have happened to the popular teenager. None of her friends had noticed any changes in her behavior in the days before she vanished and all of them insisted that Denise would never have run away from home.

On April 25, 1986, officials announced that a $5,000 reward was being offered for any information leading to Denise's whereabouts. Detectives had exhausted all leads and were hoping that the reward announcement would bring in some new tips. A month later, the reward was increased to $10,000.

Despite the monetary reward offered for information, only a few tips came in and the investigation soon stalled. Months passed, and the Pflums were forced to adjust to a new normal without Denise. Then, on August 10, 1988, they got a phone call that gave them hope that their nightmare was almost over. Judith had answered the phone and accepted a collect call from Norfolk, Virginia; the young woman on the other end of the line said she was Denise. Judith noted, "The girl said things that sounded too much like our daughter…we felt compelled to drive to Norfolk." While they were in Virginia, police in Indiana determined that the calls had been nothing but a cruel hoax. They had been made by a teenage girl who lived in Connersville. It was a huge letdown for Judith and David.

Years went by and there was no progress in finding Denise. By 2014, the case had been cold for decades but Denise's family still hoped they would one day learn what had happened to her. Judith admitted that she believed Denise was dead, but dreamed of finding her alive. "It's something you never get over. We think about it every day…the pain never goes away. You learn to wall it off and you go about your daily business."

Like detectives, Denise's family said it would have been completely out of character for her to run away from home. Judith noted, "She was an honor student, she was a talented athlete…she probably would have gotten scholarships, athletic or academic. She had so much going for her. There was no reason to run away."

Indiana State Police Detective Scott Jarvis told reporters that there had been rumors about what had happened to Denise, but few solid leads. "So far, there's not one constant theory. There isn't anyone we've focused on or any persons of interest." He admitted that solving the case grew more difficult as time passed. "Anytime this much time goes by, any potential witnesses could've died or moved on. The longer this goes on, the more rumors that come about."

Over the years, there were several rumors about Denise's fate. Some locals believed that she had witnessed something she wasn't supposed to see, like a drug deal, when she went back to the farm to look for her purse, while others thought she ran into a killer while she was on the road. Prison snitches claimed to know who was responsible for the crime and where Denise's body was buried, but the information they provided never led to the missing teenager.

The case took a surprise turn in March 2020, when detectives announced that they had arrested Denise's ex-boyfriend, Shawn McClung, and charged him with manslaughter in Denise's case. A statement provided by the Fayette County Sheriff's Office read, "The information and probable cause alleges that McClung previously claimed that Pflum was still alive, but has recently admitted that he killed her in March 1986." Shawn was in jail on unrelated charges when he was charged with Denise's murder.

Shawn had been offered a plea agreement in the case; if he provided truthful information and led authorities to Denise's body, he would be given immunity in her case and several unrelated charges would be dropped. He backed out of the deal, claiming he couldn't provide the location of Denise's body; he was then charged with voluntary manslaughter. The case was scheduled to go to trial later that year.

Unfortunately, Shawn would never go to trial in Denise's case. He had been diagnosed with a terminal illness shortly before his confession, and he died in September 2020. If he had known the location of Denise's body, he took the secret to his grave.

Denise's parents were heartbroken. In a written statement provided to reporters, they said, "We were very disappointed that he didn't give us the information we wanted but are hopeful that his attorney may be authorized to reveal more information after his death."

A few days before he died, Shawn told his lawyer that he didn't know where Denise's body was because he hadn't killed her; he claimed that he had falsely confessed to the crime because police had told him he would be able to get out of jail to be with his family if he did so. His plan fell apart when he was told that he would have to provide the location of Denise's body in order for the plea deal to take place; he told his attorney that he truly didn't know where she was and would have led police to her if it had been possible.

Denise's parents admitted that there had been several details in Shawn's confession which didn't match the facts of the case, and they had been skeptical of it from the beginning. They did, however, think that he knew more about Denise's death than he admitted.

Shawn's attorney, Judson McMillin, noted, "It is unfortunate that Mr. McClung made false statements to investigators that likely brought about a fleeting hope of closure for the Pflum family. Yet under the circumstances, where Mr. McClung's days were dwindling, his statements appear to be nothing more than a desperate attempt to live his last few days on earth as a free man."

The attorney told reporters, "Based on my own private conversations with Mr. McClung, and his overall lack of credibility, I believe the person responsible for the death or disappearance of Denise Pflum is still out there."

A spokesperson for the Fayette County Sheriff's Department noted that the investigation into Denise's disappearance was still open and active. "Our top priority is finding the truth and finally allowing the Pflum family to have the answers they have been searching for, for over 30 years. We continue to be hopeful that we will also be able to find justice for Denise Pflum."

Denise Pflum was just 18 years old when she vanished from Connersville, Indiana in March 1986. Denise was an honors student and an athlete who was looking forward to her upcoming high school graduation and planned to attend Miami University to major in microbiology. Detectives believe that she was a victim of foul play, but her body has never been found and it's possible she could still be alive. Denise has brown eyes and brown hair, and at the time of her disappearance, she was 5 feet 6 inches tall and weighed 135 pounds. She was last seen wearing a red Motley Crue T-shirt, blue striped jeans, and white sneakers; she was also wearing a gold ring with a garnet and a silver class ring with a red stone. If you have any information about Denise, please contact the Fayette County Sheriff's Department at 765-825-0535.

JAMES MARTIN ROBERTS

James Martin Roberts – known as Martin to friends and family – left his Boone, North Carolina apartment around 10:30 am on Thursday, April 21, 2016, and headed across the campus of Appalachian State University. The 19-year-old told his roommates that he was going to the library, but he when he ran into his cousin at a bus stop on the corner of Rivers Street and Blowing Rock Road, he told her he was going back to his fraternity house. He never arrived at either place and was never seen again.

Martin had been a student at Appalachian State University the previous year and joined the Tau Kappa Epsilon fraternity, but he had gotten into some trouble after he was caught drinking and driving and decided to take some time off. He moved back home to Kernersville, North Carolina for a semester, then returned to Boone and signed up for online classes at Caldwell Community College & Technical Institute. Some of his friends were unaware that he had switched schools, and Martin planned to start taking classes at Appalachian State again in the fall.

Martin's roommates were curious when he didn't return home from the library on Thursday but not particularly worried. Rod Jordan, one of his roommates, noted, "[It] wasn't too uncommon because he had other friends he stayed with." They assumed that he had spent the night elsewhere and would be back at some point on Friday.

Martin's father, John Roberts, grew concerned when he was unable to reach him on Friday and contacted his son's landlord to see if he could check on Martin. The landlord spoke with Martin's roommates, who reported that the door to his bedroom was shut and they had assumed he was inside. When they entered the room, they found all of Martin's belongings but no sign of the teenager. A note on his desk indicated that he planned to leave for a while.

The note Martin left was somewhat ambiguous but didn't state that he planned to kill himself; John said it appeared his son just wanted to "get off the grid" for a while. John was optimistic that he would see his son again at some point. "Since the note is pretty generic, it does give us hope that this is just a scenario of him not knowing what he wanted to do, just that where he was wasn't it, and he didn't know how to get out of it."

Martin's note indicated that he was disappointed in himself because he hadn't taken advantage of all the opportunities provided to him. It was possible that he had only gone to college because he believed it was what his parents wanted, and then when he didn't do well his first semester he felt guilty for letting them down. John noted, "This happens to people in all walks of life and at all ages. They get into situations they don't know how to get out of and sometimes they don't handle it the best way...they just disappear."

While the note didn't indicate that Martin was feeling suicidal, he did make it clear that he planned to make a big change in his life. Some speculated that he just wanted to go somewhere he could live off the grid, while others thought he might join the Peace Corps or some other humanitarian organization.

All of Martin's clothing, electronic devices, and other belongings had been left in his bedroom, along with his wallet and identification card. The only things missing from the apartment were some groceries he had bought shortly before he went missing. It appeared he had taken food with him, but nothing else.

Martin seemed to be in a good mood when his father last spoke to him; he sounded as if he enjoyed his classes and he mentioned applying for several jobs. His family later learned that he hadn't logged into any of his online classes for over a month and hadn't gone to any job interviews; perhaps, afraid his parents would be upset and disappointed, he decided to disappear rather than face them. According to John, Martin's note indicated that he planned on going on a journey of some kind, one that his family hoped was only temporary.

Martin was reported missing to the Boone Police Department on Friday. Investigators obtained surveillance video from the Appalcart bus Martin's cousin had gotten on, and it showed Martin walking down Rivers Street. The video lost sight of him as he approached the intersection of Rivers Street and Hardin Street; they were unable to find any further surveillance footage of the missing teen.

There was at least one witness who claimed to see Martin in the Trout Lake area of the Blue Ridge Parkway, but investigators were unable to confirm this sighting. Martin was known to spend a lot of time hiking on the trails around the Blue Ridge Parkway, so it seemed plausible that he might have headed there. Investigators conducted a search of the area using a North Carolina State Police helicopter equipped with infrared radar but found no sign of Martin.

A friend of the family referred to Martin as "a good kid who lost his way." He was normally a very social person, but he had been more serious about his studies when he returned after his semester off and his roommates had no idea that he hadn't been going to class.

Martin and a group of friends, including Holly Nicholson, had gone to a local café the Tuesday before he vanished to take part in a trivia night. Holly hadn't noticed anything unusual about Martin's behavior at the time. "He was a funny guy, he made lots of jokes. Everybody loved hanging out with him and he made everyone smile."

Martin's mother, Abby, said that it was out of character for Martin to vanish without contacting anyone and she feared for his safety. "It just hurts to think that he doesn't know how much he is loved." She hoped he would see the outpouring of support from friends, family, and complete strangers and realize how much he was missed.

John said he couldn't think about anything other than finding his son. "This situation is very unusual, very strange, very unexpected. Martin has never had any kind of situation where he just left and has been alone like this. We didn't see it coming and had no clue that anything like this could possibly happen." He was hopeful that someone in Boone might have seen Martin and could provide clues to his whereabouts.

Detectives said that there was nothing in Martin's note that led them to believe that he was going to harm himself, so they were treating the case as a standard missing person case. They interviewed bus drivers but didn't find any who recalled picking Martin up, leading them to believe that he had left campus on foot. Dozens of volunteers, including many of Martin's fraternity brothers, assisted in searching the area around campus for any sign of the missing student.

Martin had left all his belongings – including his cell phone – in his room, and his father didn't believe he had access to much cash. It was possible someone had given him a ride or money, perhaps not knowing that he was a missing person. Detectives asked anyone who believed they had interacted with him to contact them. They stressed that they just wanted to know that Martin was safe; although his family desperately wanted him to come home, detectives noted that he was an adult and they would not reveal his whereabouts if he didn't want them to.

Investigators said that they received numerous tips in the days following Martin's disappearance and followed up on each one. Boone Police Capt. Andy Le Beau noted. "We've been trying to base searches off of intelligence we gather. When we hear of an area where there possibly was a sighting, we go and search that area." Unfortunately, they hadn't found any clues to Martin's whereabouts.

As days went by, Martin's loved ones grew increasingly desperate to hear from him. They feared that he might have gone on a hike to clear his head and then had some kind of accident on the trail. Family members were staying in Boone to assist in the search, going out each day and scouring the area for any sign of Martin. They were unable to find any trace of him. John admitted, "Unfortunately, there's a lot of different ways he could have gone, a lot of different places he could be."

Two weeks after Martin vanished, officials announced that they were expanding their search area. Areas throughout North Carolina had been searched, as well as parts of Virginia and South Carolina. Missing person flyers had been posted along the Appalachian Trail and other outdoor areas Martin might be drawn to. Boone Police Chief Dana Crawford stated, "We owe it to his family to look under every rock, turn every page that we can possibly turn, to develop something. Somebody, somewhere, knows something."

Crime Stoppers announced that they were offering a $1,000 reward for information leading to Martin's location, and investigators hoped that this would bring in some new leads. As days turned into weeks, however, they admitted that they had no idea where Martin might have gone.

A month after Martin was last seen, investigators were still trying to piece together what he had been doing in the days and hours leading up to his disappearance. They had been unable to account for several large chunks of his time, and they believed that he might have been with someone who knew where he could be found. Capt. Le Beau stated, "Martin was spending time with somebody here in the High Country area. There are certain amounts of time out of his day that are unaccounted for and we know that somebody knows about this...we would love to speak to you. It can be private, we just need the information."

On June 1, 2016, a search team scoured Trout Lake for any sign of Martin. Although his family wanted to believe he was still alive, they recognized that there was a chance he wasn't and this search was focused on looking for his body. John noted, "All [other] efforts have been under the assumption that he's out there somewhere and we can find him, whether it's an injury, an accident, or he's just taken some time off to be by himself." Now, cadaver dogs were used to scan the area for any hint of decomposition. The search came up empty.

John's birthday came and went without any contact from his son; those who knew Martin well had been sure he would call his father to wish him a happy birthday and his failure to do so left them feeling even more desperate to learn what had happened to him. John had noted, "The best birthday present in the world would be to hear from him that he's okay, and that he's safe, whether he's ready to come home now or later." He was saddened by the lack of contact.

As the search for Martin passed the two-month mark, investigators asked members of the public to be on the alert as they opened their vacation homes up for the summer. Capt. Le Beau stated, "He could've broken into a vacation home and been living off their pantry for a while. We are doing everything we can, but the frustrating part is that we come up with nothing. We are still banging our heads against the wall."

Unsure where else to look, Boone Police Detective Kevin Wilson consulted with experts at the National Center for Missing and Exploited Children. "While the NCMEC investigators were pleased with the amount of work we have accomplished, they were able to come up with some new ideas and offer services that we do not have available on a local level. They will offer continual support to our investigation."

Martin should have been celebrating his 20th birthday on August 19, 1996, and his mother marked the occasion by baking a cake for him. She made an appeal on Facebook for him to contact her and let her know he was okay – even if he didn't want to return home.

Months went by and there was little progress on the case. On the first anniversary of Martin's disappearance, detectives decided to go back over the entire case file to see if they might have missed something. Over the course of the investigation, they had served 35 search warrants in order to access things like Martin's bank accounts, cell phone records, and email accounts. None of them had been accessed since Martin went missing and they provided no useful information.

Years passed and Martin's case went cold. On the fifth anniversary of his disappearance, detectives admitted that they had conducted dozens of searches for the missing student but were no closer to finding out what had happened to him. Although they were still receiving tips on a weekly basis, they hadn't been able to develop any solid leads and there had been no confirmed sightings of Martin since he walked down Rivers Street after speaking with his cousin. His trail ended within blocks of his apartment.

    Martin's loved ones tried to remain optimistic that they would see him again one day. His father stated, "We still have hope because we don't have a reason not to hope."

    James Martin Roberts was just 19 years old when he went missing from Boone, North Carolina in April 2016. Martin left a note behind indicating that he wanted to get away for a while; he also expressed regret for not taking advantage of all the opportunities he had been given. Detectives have stopped short of calling it a suicide note as there was no indication Martin wanted to harm himself. Martin has blue eyes and brown hair, and at the time of his disappearance, he was 5 feet 10 inches tall and weighed 145 pounds. He has a Bob Marley quote tattooed on his right ribcage and one of red, blue, and black mountains on his left forearm. He was last seen wearing khaki shorts, a black shirt, an Appalachian State University windbreaker, white socks, gray New Balance sneakers, and a white visor. If you have any information about Martin, please contact the Boone Police Department at 828-268-6900.

DOROTHY SCOFIELD

Dorothy Scofield and her mother left their Citra, Florida home on the morning of Thursday, July 22, 1976, and headed to the J. M. Fields Plaza in Ocala, Florida. While Dorothy's mother went into the Florida Highway Patrol office to renew her driver's license, the 12-year-old went into the J. M. Fields department store to exchange a pair of sandals. Dorothy – known as Deedee to family and friends – was seen browsing in a couple of the stores in the shopping mall, but she failed to meet her mother at the designated time and she was never seen again.

Deedee's mother, Lena Scofield, called the Ocala Police Department and reported her daughter missing that afternoon; she told investigators that Deedee had no history of running away and wasn't having any problems at home. She stated that Deedee had wanted to buy her older brother a birthday present at the shopping mall, and Lena had allowed her to go by herself because she was going to be right next door. "It was the first time I had ever let her go anywhere on her own."

Ocala Police Detective Gordon Welch questioned employees who worked in the shopping mall but none of them were able to provide any clues to Deedee's location. The last sighting of her had been around 2:00 pm, when she was seen buying a watch band for her brother in J.M. Fields department store. Detective Welch noted, "After that point, we have nothing. There was no commotion in the parking lot, no one even saw her leave the store. She's just gone."

Police searched the area surrounding the shopping mall on foot and by helicopter, but they didn't find anything related to Deedee's disappearance. Officials with the Ocala Police Department asked for the assistance of the FBI due to the possibility that Deedee had been kidnapped.

Detective Welch stated that investigators were considering the possibility that Deedee's disappearance was linked to the robbery that had taken place in Ocala National Forest the previous month, but admitted, "We have no firm evidence connecting the two incidents…it's a pretty slim hope."

A week after Deedee was last seen, her family announced that they were offering a $1,000 reward for information leading to her safe return. They had also consulted with a psychic after learning that police had run out of leads to follow. Ocala Police Chief Lee McGehee stated that investigators had no idea what had happened to the missing girl. "We're trying to determine now why she's gone." Although detectives were open to the possibility that Deedee had run away, they admitted that it would be out of character for her to do so and they were leaning towards foul play.

A motel in Ocala offered to let Deedee's family stay there for free while they were taking part in the search for the little girl. Ocala residents who had never met the family showed up at the motel to provide meals for the Scofields and assist them in the search. A local print shop made 5,000 copies of Deedee's missing flyer and reward posters so volunteers could distribute them throughout the area.

On Saturday, July 31, 1976, Deedee's family received a phone call from someone who claimed to have the little girl. Deedee's brother-in-law, Ron Scott, answered the phone and heard a low voice say, "If you want your daughter back, go to the following address..." Scott quickly wrote the address down, but the caller hung up before he could ask any questions. His wife, Tori, immediately called the phone company, hoping they could trace the call, but they were unable to provide any help.

Tori called the Ocala Police Department and asked to speak to one of the detectives assigned to Deedee's case, but none of them were available at the time. Frustrated, Deedee's father, Joseph Scofield, decided to drive to the address himself. Ron offered to accompany him, and the two men took off, hoping to return with Deedee.

When the men got to the address, they discovered the call had been nothing more than a cruel hoax. "It was just two families arguing. One wanted to get the other in trouble." It was a huge disappointment for Deedee's family members, and Lena broke into tears when she found out. "God, I can't believe the stuff some people pull."

Joseph vowed that he was going to keep searching for his daughter despite the setback. "I'm going to keep plugging. I'll go until the money runs out. I won't quit...I'll spend all I have to get her back."

Deedee and her family had moved to Florida from Hilliard, Ohio the previous autumn. Deedee was enrolled in North Marion Elementary School, where she had no problems making friends. She was an honor student and always brought home excellent grades, and her sister described her as "exceptional, really a sweet person."

Although Deedee's parents told detectives that the 12-year-old hadn't had any problems adjusting to life in Florida, some of her friends at school said that Deedee had mentioned missing Ohio and wanted to move back to her old home town. Investigators considered the possibility that Deedee had decided to run away to Ohio, but none of her friends there had spoken to her and were unaware of her desire to move back.

Deedee's sisters, Toni and Shelly, were adamant that Deedee was not a runaway. Toni insisted, "She is not the type." She was too close with her parents and siblings to even consider running away from home.

As news of Deedee's disappearance spread, detectives heard from a convenience store clerk who worked at a store 15 miles away from the shopping mall where Deedee was last seen. The clerk told investigators that a young girl matching Deedee's description had come into the store around 2:30 pm the day she was reported missing. The girl, who looked like she had been crying, bought some soft drinks and then got into a car driven by an unidentified male. It was the last reported sighting of Deedee, though police admitted that they couldn't confirm that it had been Deedee who had been at the convenience store.

On August 3, 1976, Deedee's family announced that the reward for information was being raised to $2,000. Her father told reporters that he hoped the increased reward would bring in some new tips, as detectives had exhausted all leads and still had no idea what had happened to Deedee.

Joe and Lena stated that they had put much of what they owned up for sale to finance the search for their daughter. They hired a private investigator, spoke with psychics from as far away as Europe, and asked every police agency in the area for help. Joe noted, "All I want to do is get her back. I don't care what it costs. Whatever I have is for sale. And I will continue until I exhaust what we have."

Lena said she knew in her heart that Deedee was not a runaway. "A child who comes up and kisses mommy and daddy on the cheek and tells them she loves them is not going to run away." She described her daughter as someone who loved going to church and was the kind of person who liked to plan everything out ahead of time. She was far too sensible to run away without taking any clothing or money with her.

Jane Kershner, one of Deedee's teachers, also thought it was unlikely she was a runaway. "She is the kind of child who thinks things out before she does it. I doubt seriously she would have left without money or clothes. She is a very bright, careful child, an excellent student with above average intelligence. She had top grades, was interested in everything, and spent her time helping other students."

Sgt. Welch admitted that investigators had been unable to find any trace of Deedee. "Despite the man hours put into this case, we still have nothing to indicate whether she was abducted or she ran away. We have one fact: she's missing."

Lena couldn't bring herself to leave the house. Instead, she spent each day sitting by the telephone, praying that she would hear from her daughter. "When the phone rings, you get your hopes up before you even answer it. That's why I stay here. I feel Deedee will call if she can."

By the end of August, Deedee was still missing and police were still at a loss to explain what had happened to her. Her family told reporters that they had been touched by the number of strangers who reached out to them to offer their support; they had received cards and letters from people from as far away as Wisconsin and California. Many of the letter-writers just wanted the family to know they were praying for them, but one was from a Florida detective agency that offered to work on the case free of charge.

Weeks turned into months, and Deedee's fate remained a mystery. By the end of the year, it was clear the case was starting to go cold. Sgt. Welch stated that investigators had followed up on every tip they received, but nothing brought them any closer to finding Deedee. "It's just going to take patience, that's all." He told reporters that despite the lack of evidence, detectives had ruled out the possibility that Deedee was a runaway. "She's not that type of girl. I just don't believe she would do anything like that."

Sgt. Welch traveled to Daytona Beach after a man reported seeing a young woman he believed was Deedee at a home there. When he knocked on the door of the house in question, Sgt. Welch thought for a minute that his search was over. "I almost had a heart attack...it was Dee, right down to the wire-rimmed glasses." The young woman could have been Deedee's twin, but it wasn't Deedee. Sgt. Welch returned to Ocala empty-handed.

Deedee should have been celebrating her 13th birthday on January 8, 1977. Lena spent the day at home, crying whenever she thought of her missing daughter. She told reporters that she was still optimistic that Deedee would be found safely. "I can see no reason why we can't continue hoping as long as there's been nothing found or any other kind of news."

In July 1977, the Scofield family marked the grim first anniversary of Deedee's disappearance. They were convinced that Deedee was still alive, and they were desperate to find her. Joe said he knew that Deedee hadn't run away, but he almost wished that she had. "I'd get down on my knees and kiss the ground if I really thought that's what happened." The alternatives were too horrible to think about.

Joe had done everything possible over the past year to find his daughter, but he admitted that he hadn't had any luck chasing down leads. "Everything we tried came to a dead end. We've never even had a confirmed sighting."

Florida Highway Patrol Sgt. Robert Howard had been at the Highway Patrol office when Lena went in to renew her license. He had taken part in the initial search for Deedee, and told reporters that he often thought about the missing child. "Since it happened right here under our noses, I think about it a lot. It makes you afraid to let a child out of a car at a shopping center."

Like the other investigators, Sgt. Howard said he didn't believe that Deedee left voluntarily. "There is always the possibility when you're dealing with a 12-year-old child that it's a runaway, but I think the chances are greater that she was abducted."

Deedee's disappearance took a huge toll on her parents. They sold the small barbeque restaurant they owned to finance the search; when the money from that sale ran out, they sold their property. When they ran out of funds, they borrowed money. Despite everything they tried, however, Deedee's location remained a mystery.

By 1982, Deedee had been missing for six years and Joe and Lena's marriage had disintegrated. Lena remained in Florida and told reporters she would never stop looking for her youngest child. "I don't know if you ever adjust. It has torn everybody up. We always had a happy family life. We always had a good time. You cry a lot and you pray a lot. After that, there's nothing left."

In October 1983, the Florida Department of Law Enforcement released an age-progression photo of

Deedee, showing what she might look like as a 19-year-old. They based the composite off of photographs of Deedee, her mother, and her older sisters. A spokesperson for the department hoped that the photo would bring in some new tips that might finally lead investigators to Deedee. "There's no worse agony in the world than not knowing where your children are."

The Ocala Police Department has never stopped searching for Deedee, but they haven't had any new leads in years. In July 2022, they released a new age-progression photograph of Deedee and asked for anyone with any information to contact detectives. Unfortunately, Deedee's parents died without ever learning what had happened to their youngest child, but Deedee's siblings continue to look for her.

Dorothy Delilah Scofield was just 12 years old when she went missing from Ocala, Florida in July 1976. Deedee was an excellent student and made friends easily, and she was very close with her parents and siblings. Detectives believe that Deedee was abducted and likely murdered, but her body has never been found. Deedee has blue eyes and brown hair, and at the time of her disappearance, she was 4 feet 11 inches tall and weighed 90 pounds. She was last seen wearing blue jeans, a red body suit with a blue flower design, a button-up shirt, a brown leather belt, and lime-green high-top Keds sneakers. She had a mole on her knee and needed eyeglasses to see. If you have any information about Deedee, please contact the Ocala Police Department at 352-629-8508.

CARLENE TENGELSEN

Carlene Tengelsen had recently gotten her driver's license and had never driven anywhere, so she was thrilled when her mother allowed her to use the family car to pick up her younger sister from summer camp on Wednesday, June 21, 1972. The 16-year-old left her home in Macon, Georgia in the early afternoon, intending to stop by a local shopping plaza before heading to Mercer University, where her sister was on a field trip with her camp group. Carlene invited her younger brother and older sister to come with her, but neither was interested and the teenager left alone in the white 1963 station wagon. She never returned home and she was never seen again.

The first sign that something was wrong came around 4:00 pm, when 14-year-old Joanette Tengelsen called home asking why no one had picked her up from summer camp. At first, Joan Tengelsen told her younger daughter that she was sure Carlene would be there any minute and to just sit tight. After more than an hour passed, Joanette called home again. Carlene still hadn't picked her up and she was getting bored of waiting. Eventually, 17-year-old Arnelle Tengelsen drove to Mercer University and picked up her youngest sister.

Joan Tengelsen wasn't sure what to think when Carlene failed to pick up Joanette and didn't return home that afternoon. Although Carlene had only had her driver's license for about a week, she was normally a very responsible teenager and it was unlike her to go anywhere without letting someone know. As hours went by without any sign of Carlene, Joan started to worry that something might have happened to her.

Carlene's father, Arnold, was on a business trip in Florida at the time the teenager went missing. Although Joan was initially reluctant to worry him, as darkness fell without any word from Carlene, she called him and told him that the teenager was missing. He had just checked into a hotel in Deland, Florida, more than five hours away from home. Despite a brewing hurricane, Arnold immediately left the hotel and headed for Macon, driving as fast as he could on the rain-soaked highway.

Joan called the Macon Police Department and reported Carlene missing, but they didn't take the case seriously at first. Since Carlene was a teenager, they assumed that she had simply gone off with some of her friends and would return home when she was ready. Although they did spend a few hours searching for the Pontiac station wagon Carlene had been driving, they were unable to locate it.

Arnelle was supposed to go out with her boyfriend, Marvin, that night. She canceled the date so she could help her mother search for Carlene; they started calling all of the teenager's friends, trying to find someone who might know where she could be. Wanting to help, Marvin picked up Joanette and the two of them spent hours driving around Macon, searching in vain for any sign of Carlene or the white station wagon.

The first place they searched was the Westgate Shopping Center, where Carlene planned to stop on her way to pick up Joanette. Her family was able to confirm that Carlene had made it to the shopping center that afternoon; some teenage boys she knew from school had been playing pinball at Newberry's and they said that Carlene had stopped and watched them play for a while.

After leaving the pinball machines, Carlene then headed to the shopping center located behind Westgate; her boyfriend had been working at the Winn-Dixie supermarket that day and she left a note for him on the windshield of his car. He hadn't seen Carlene but found the note when he finished his shift. "Came by to see you...see you tonight." By that night, however, Carlene was gone.

Joanette and Marvin drove around Macon until well after midnight. They had driven through countless parking lots and dozens of side streets, but Carlene and the white Pontiac were nowhere to be found. Around 1:45 am, they made a final pass through the Westgate Shopping Center as they headed for home. Suddenly, in the parking lot across from Krispy Kreme, Joanette spotted the white station wagon.

At first, Joanette could only stare at the car in shock. She and Marvin had searched this same parking lot earlier, and the car definitely hadn't been there at that time. Marvin pointed out that there was a Macon police car in the same parking lot; although the entire police force was aware of Carlene's disappearance and officers were supposed to be on the lookout for the white station wagon, the officer hadn't noticed that he was only feet away from the wanted vehicle.

Marvin approached the police officer and asked him if he was searching for a white Pontiac station wagon. When the cop confirmed that he was, Marvin pointed it out. "Well, it's sitting right over there." Although the car had been located, Carlene was still nowhere to be found.

When the Pontiac was found, the driver's side door was ajar and the windows were down. Joan was adamant that her daughter never would have left the car in that condition; she had been taught to always make sure the car's windows were rolled up and the doors were locked whenever she got out of the vehicle. "Carlene would not have left it like that." She knew that she risked losing her driving privileges if she didn't take good care of the family's car.

Despite the fact that Carlene hadn't been found with the car, police still insisted that she was likely off with friends and there was no need for concern. Arnold, however, insisted that something was wrong. He was certain his daughter hadn't been the person who abandoned the station wagon; he feared she had been a victim of foul play and her abductor had later ditched the vehicle where it was found. Arnold pleaded with police to process the Pontiac for evidence. They finally dusted it for fingerprints but found nothing useful.

Joan told reporters that there was no way Carlene would have voluntarily abandoned her family. She was close with her parents and siblings; she and Joanette shared a bedroom, and though they would sometimes fight over the space – Joanette liked to keep things neat while Carlene could be somewhat messy – they had a close bond and didn't keep secrets from each other.

Carlene's younger brother, Tom, was small for his age and sometimes got picked on by some of the older boys in the neighborhood. Carlene was fiercely protective of Tom; he knew that all he had to do was yell for her when he was getting picked on and she would drop whatever she was doing and run to his defense.

Shortly before she went missing, Carlene finished her sophomore year of high school at Southwest High School in Macon. She had always done well in school; she got along well with her classmates and never gave her teachers any problems. She had a steady boyfriend – she had been wearing his class ring when she vanished – and had been looking forward to a date with him on the night she went missing. Joan noted, "She's never done anything like this before. She never spent a night away from home and was always home on time from her dates." In her mother's eyes, foul play was the only explanation for Carlene's disappearance.

The Tengelsen family flooded the area with missing person posters and made sure that Carlene's picture was displayed in all area businesses. Carlene's friends and classmates spent hours driving throughout Macon, handing out flyers and searching for any sign of the missing teenager.

Two weeks after Carlene vanished, her family announced that they were offering a $500 reward for information leading to her whereabouts. While the Macon Police Department and the Macon-Bibb County Civil Defense Office were both officially investigating the disappearance, detectives believed that Carlene had most likely left the area voluntarily and they still expected her to return home eventually.

Joan was devastated by the disappearance of her daughter. She alternated between weeks of sleepless nights and months when she didn't want to get out of bed. She refused to leave the house, fearing that someone would call about Carlene the moment she stepped away from the phone. For six weeks, she slept in her clothes, wanting to make sure she would be ready to leave immediately if she got a phone call that Carlene had been found.

The family received dozens of calls, but they were mostly from people who provided only vague information yet hoped to collect the reward money. Others were clearly in need of mental help; one woman insisted that Carlene lived in her attic and would come down each night to steal food from her refrigerator.

Months went by and Carlene's fate remained a mystery. Although the teenager remained listed as a missing person, Macon police did little to try and find her. The investigation was hindered by the fact that officers initially believed that Carlene had run away from home; by the time they were willing to admit that she could have been a victim of foul play, the case was already ice cold.

In May 1973, Joan told Arnold that she didn't want to live in Macon anymore. She was haunted by memories of her missing daughter and thought it would be good to have a change of scenery. Arnold arranged to buy a steakhouse in Durham, North Carolina, and moved his family there.

Before leaving Georgia, Joan arranged for their neighbors to have a second phone line installed; the phone number that had belonged to the Tengelsens was transferred over to this phone line so that Carlene would still have a way to call home if she were able. The neighbors kept the phone number active for three years; in 1977, the Tengelsens moved back to Macon.

In July 1981, Arnold filed a petition to have Carlene declared legally dead. On August 26, 1981, a Bibb County judge ruled that the legal presumption of death had been established and granted Arnold's petition. Carlene had been missing for more than nine years at that point and there had never been any confirmed sightings of her. Although it didn't change her case status with the Macon police – she remained listed as a missing person – her family had accepted the fact that she had likely been killed on the same night that she vanished.

Although they never got over the loss of Carlene, Joan and Arnold refused to allow their grief to completely consume them. They would still talk about her often, especially late at night when it was just the two of them, but they resigned themselves to the fact that they might never get answers about what had happened to her. In 2004, shortly after the couple celebrated their 50th wedding anniversary, Arnold died at the age of 78. Joan liked to think that Carlene was waiting for him in heaven.

In 2009, Joan noted that current missing children cases were treated far differently than they had been in the 1970s. The pain felt by parents, however, remained the same. "Anytime I see on the news that a child is missing, I pray for that family…I feel a kinship with them because I know the hell that they're gonna go through…it's something so horrible that you can't really express it."

Joan said that if she were able to speak to the person responsible for her daughter's disappearance, she would ask them why they did it – and she would tell them that she forgave them. Her faith had grown stronger over the years and she was looking for answers, not vengeance. Joan died in December 2016 at the age of 83, hopefully finally getting the answers she so desperately wanted.

June 2022 marked the 50th anniversary of Carlene's disappearance. In the five decades since she vanished, her parents and her older sister had died, but Joanette and Tom still hoped to learn what had happened to her. Joanette stated, "People say, 'After 50 years, you know she's dead,' and I know that's probably true. I just don't want to say I agree and that's it. I just can't let it go…it would be nice to know for sure, to have some justice to it."

Joanette wasn't as willing as her mother to blindly forgive the person who stole her sister away from her. "I hate that person, and I've had to ask God to forgive me for hating them, because I don't even know who they are." She hopes she can one day forgive this person, but noted that if she ever met them face-to-face, "I may not be so nice."

Carlene Sessions Tengelsen was just 16 years old when she vanished from Macon, Georgia in June 1972. She had just finished her sophomore year of high school and had only had her driver's license for a week when she went missing; although police initially believed she was a runaway, those close to her knew that she would never have voluntarily walked away from her family. Carlene has hazel eyes and brown hair, and at the time of her disappearance, she was 5 feet 9 inches tall and weighed 115 pounds. Although her hair was naturally curly, she preferred to iron it straight. Carlene was last seen wearing blue jeans with metal studs down the sides and one of her dad's blue button-down shirts; she also had on her Mickey Mouse watch, a silver POW bracelet engraved with the name of an American soldier taken prisoner during the Vietnam War, and her boyfriend's white gold class ring. She had braces on her teeth when she went missing. If you have any information about Carlene, please contact the Macon Police Department at 912-751-7505.

Printed in Great Britain
by Amazon